lighthouse 1
BASIC
Grammarmaster

Deinen Grammarmaster findest du auch in der **Cornelsen Lernen App**.

Siehst du eines dieser Symbole in deinem Grammarmaster, findest du in der App …

- alle **Audios**
- alle **Erklärfilme**
- **Lösungen** zu den Aufgaben

Cornelsen

BASIC
lighthouse 1

Grammarmaster

Im Auftrag des Verlages erarbeitet von
Gwen Berwick, York
Sydney Thorne, York

In Zusammenarbeit mit der Englischredaktion
Klaus Unger (Projektleitung), Anja Zieschang

Beratende Mitwirkung
Daniel Henn, Frankfurt/Main; Christina Sieber, Schorndorf

Lizenzmanagement
Silke Kirchhoff

Illustrationen
Evelt Yanait, Advocate Art

Fotos
Anja Poehlmann, Brighton
Für die freundliche Unterstützung danken wir der
Varndean School, Brighton

Umschlaggestaltung
Rosendahl, Berlin

Layoutkonzept
Klein & Halm, Berlin

Layout und technische Umsetzung
Straive

Druck
AZ Druck und Datentechnik GmbH, Kempten

PEFC-zertifiziert
Dieses Produkt stammt aus nachhaltig bewirtschafteten Wäldern und kontrollierten Quellen
PEFC/04-31-2260 www.pefc.de

www.cornelsen.de

Soweit in diesem Lehrwerk Personen fotografisch abgebildet sind und ihnen von der Redaktion fiktive Namen, Berufe, Dialoge und Ähnliches zugeordnet oder diese Personen in bestimmte Kontexte gesetzt werden, dienen diese Zuordnungen und Darstellungen ausschließlich der Veranschaulichung und dem besseren Verständnis des Buchinhaltes.

Dieses Werk berücksichtigt die Regeln der reformierten Rechtschreibung und Zeichensetzung.

Die Webseiten Dritter, deren Internetadressen in diesem Lehrwerk angegeben sind, wurden vor Drucklegung sorgfältig geprüft. Der Verlag übernimmt keine Gewähr für die Aktualität und den Inhalt dieser Seiten oder solcher, die mit ihnen verlinkt sind.

Alle Drucke dieser Auflage sind inhaltlich unverändert und können im Unterricht nebeneinander verwendet werden.

© 2023 Cornelsen Verlag GmbH, Berlin

Das Werk und seine Teile sind urheberrechtlich geschützt. Jede Nutzung in anderen als den gesetzlich zugelassenen Fällen bedarf der vorherigen schriftlichen Einwilligung des Verlages.

Hinweis zu §§ 60 a, 60 b UrhG: Weder das Werk noch seine Teile dürfen ohne eine solche Einwilligung an Schulen oder in Unterrichts- und Lehrmedien (§ 60 b Abs. 3 UrhG) vervielfältigt, insbesondere kopiert oder eingescannt, verbreitet oder in ein Netzwerk eingestellt oder sonst öffentlich zugänglich gemacht oder wiedergegeben werden. Dies gilt auch für Intranets von Schulen.

1. Auflage, 1. Druck 2023
978-3-06-034634-9

Inhalt

So lernst du mit Lighthouse	U2
Impressum	2
Inhaltsverzeichnis	3

Unit 1
My new school

Der unbestimmte Artikel: *a/an*	4
A/an vor Vokalen	5
Der bestimmte Artikel: *the*	5
Der Plural der Nomen	6
Der Plural der Nomen: Formen	7
Die Personalpronomen	8
Das Verb *be*: Bejahte Aussagesätze	10
Das Verb *be*: Verneinte Aussagesätze	12
Der s-Genitiv	14
Die *of*-Fügung	15

Unit 2
My family and home

Das Verb *be*: Fragen und Kurzantworten	17
There is … / There are …	20
Possessivbegleiter	21

Unit 3
My day

Das simple present: Bejahte Aussagesätze	23
Das simple present: Sonderformen	26
Die Wortstellung	27

Unit 4
Where I live

Das simple present: Verneinte Aussagesätze	46
Das simple present: Fragen und Kurzantworten	50
Das simple present: Fragen mit Fragewörtern	52

Unit 5
Enjoy!

Das present progressive: Bejahte Aussagesätze	55
Die *ing*-Form: Schreibung	56
Das present progressive: Verneinte Aussagesätze	57
Das present progressive: Fragen	58
much – many – a lot of	60

Auf einen Blick — 64

Lösungen	29
Quellenverzeichnis	72

Unit 1
My new school

> **Der unbestimmte Artikel: *a/an***
>
> Der unbestimmte Artikel (ein, eine) heißt im Englischen **a** oder **an**.
> Du verwendest
> - **a**, wenn das folgende Wort mit einem Konsonanten (b, c, d, ..., z) beginnt,
>   *a boy* – ein Junge   *a car* – ein Auto
> - **an**, wenn das folgende Wort mit einem Vokal (a, e, i, o, u) beginnt.
>   *an animal* – ein Tier   *an exercise book* – ein Heft
>
> ❗ Substantive (*boy, car, rabbit*) schreibst du (anders als im Deutschen) klein.
>
> ▶ SB p. 21, p. 175

1 T-shirts

a) **What's on the T-shirt? Circle *a* or *an*.**
   Was ist auf dem T-Shirt? Kreise a *oder* an *ein.*

   an: wenn das folgende Wort mit A, E, I, O, U beginnt

a / an lion

a / an horse

a / an elephant

a / an seagull

a / an apple

a / an orange

a / an hat

a / an bike

b) **Write *a* or *an*.** *Schreibe* a *oder* an.

   1 ____ horse is ____ animal.

   2 You can eat ____ apple.

   3 I can see ____ zebra, ____ gorilla and ____ orang utan.

Zebra, gorilla und *orang utan* sind neue Wörter, aber keine Angst! Du weißt nun über *a* und *an* Bescheid, und kannst das richtige Wort einsetzen.

▶ Check

> **A/an vor Vokalen**
>
> Vorsicht bei vorgeschobenen Adjektiven, die mit einem Vokal (a, e, i, o, u) beginnen.
> *I have a dog. It's an old dog. – Ich habe einen Hund. Er ist ein alter Hund.*
>
> Bei der Wahl von **a** oder **an** ist die **Aussprache** entscheidend, nicht die Schreibweise, also:
>   *a uniform – eine Uniform*   ... weil das gesprochene Wort am Anfang
>   *a unit – eine Lerneinheit*   wie *you* klingt
> Aber: *an hour – eine Stunde*   ... weil das „h" am Anfang nicht gesprochen wird
>
> ▶ SB p. 21, p. 175

2 At school

a) Read the sentences in 2b). In the underlined words, highlight the first letter in red if it is a vowel (A, E, I, O, U) and in blue if it is a consonant. *Lies die Sätze in 2b). Markiere den ersten Buchstaben der unterstrichenen Wörter in Rot, wenn es ein Vokal ist (A, E, I, O, U) und in Blau, wenn es ein Konsonant ist.*

b) (Circle) the right word: *a* or *an*. *Kreise das richtige Wort ein:* a *oder* an.

  1 I have a / an book. It's a / an big book. It's a / an English book.

  2 And I have a / an pencil. It's a / an old pencil, but I like it.

  3 I have a / an exercise book. It's a / an orange exercise book.

> **Der bestimmte Artikel: *the***
>
> Du sprichst den **bestimmten Artikel the** (der, die, das):
> • [ðə], vor einem Wort, das mit einem Konsonanten beginnt: *the [ðə] teacher, the [ðə] car*
> • [ði], vor einem Wort, das mit einem Vokal (a, e, i, o, u) beginnt: *the [ði] animal, the [ði] apple*
>
> ▶ SB p. 21, p. 175

3 Mr Lee's sentences

a) Read the sentences in 3b). In the underlined words, highlight the first letter in red if it is a vowel (A, E, I, O, U) and in blue if it is a consonant. *Lies die Sätze in 3b). Markiere den ersten Buchstaben der unterstrichenen Wörter in Rot, wenn es ein Vokal ist (A, E, I, O, U) und in Blau, wenn es ein Konsonant ist.*

b) Then tick the right column: [ðə] or [ði]. *Hake die richtige Spalte ab:* [ðə] *oder* [ði].

	ðə	ði
1 Look at the board!	✓	
2 Open the book at page 21.		
3 Eat the apple, please.		
4 Listen to the English students.		

🔊 c) Now read the sentences aloud. Take care with 'the'. *Lies die Sätze laut vor. Achte auf „the".*   ▶ Check

1

Der Plural der Nomen

An die meisten Nomen wird im Plural -s angehängt.

a dog → *two dogs* – ein Hund, zwei Hunde

a cat → *three cats* – eine Katze, drei Katzen

❗ Sonderformen:
one child → two children – Kind / Kinder
one man → two men – Mann / Männer
one woman → two women – Frau / Frauen

Ein paar wenige Nomen haben keine Singularform und werden nur im Plural gebraucht:
people – Menschen   *trousers* – Hose   *clothes* – Kleidung

▶ SB p. 22, p. 175

4 Sunita is at the zoo

Write the correct words in the plural.
Schreibe die Wörter im Plural.

child • ~~elephant~~ • lion • man • parrot • snake • woman

I can see two *elephants*_____, three _____, four _____,

five _____, six _____, seven _____

and eight _____.

▶ Check

Der Plural der Nomen: Formen

Die Folgenden sind die drei wichtigsten Pluralformen:

1. die meisten Nomen + -s
   a lion → two lions
   a year → three years

2. -s, -x, -ch oder -sh + -es
   a bus → two buses
   a beach → two beaches

3. Vokal + y + -s
   a boy → two boys

   Konsonant + y wird zu -ies
   a story → two stories
   a pony → two ponies   ▶ SB p. 22, p. 175

5 Words with -y

a) Look at the words in **5b)**. Highlight the underlined letters: blue for a consonant, red for a vowel (A, E, I, O, U). *Schau dir die Wörter in 5b) an. Markiere die unterstrichenen Buchstaben: blau für einen Konsonanten, rot für einen Vokal (A, E, I, O, U).*

b) Write the correct plural forms in Amira's poster: *-s* or *-ies*. *Schreibe die richtigen Pluralformen in Amiras Poster: -s oder -ies.*

1 h o l i d a y
2 h o b b y
3 m o n k e y
4 p o n y

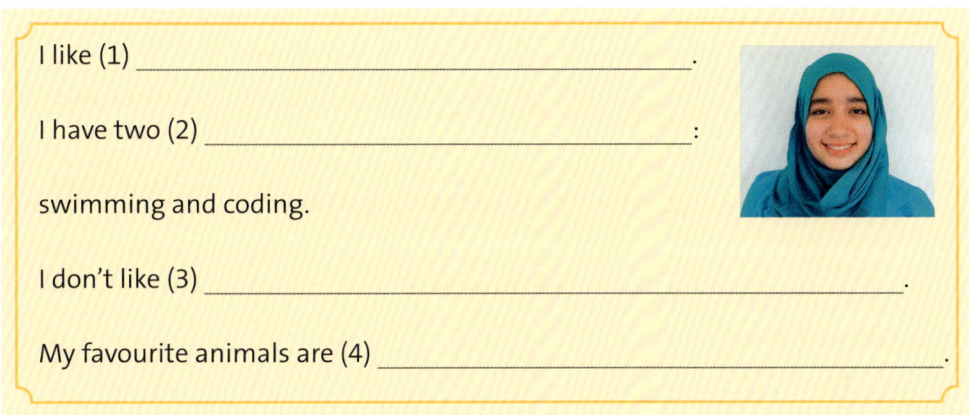

I like (1) _____ .

I have two (2) _____ :

swimming and coding.

I don't like (3) _____ .

My favourite animals are (4) _____ .

6 More than one

a) Look again at the grammar box. Then read the highlighted words in **6b)**. Are they in group 1, 2, or 3? *Schau dir den Grammatikkasten noch einmal an. Lies dann die markierten Wörter in 6b). Gehören sie zu Gruppe 1, 2 oder 3?*

b) Complete the sentences with the plural of the words.
Vervollständige die Sätze mit dem Plural der Wörter.

1 friend   _1_   Hassan and Sasha are my _____ .

2 baby   ____ I love _____ .

3 box   ____ Look at the words in the two _____ .

4 sandwich ____ I eat _____ at school.

5 pen, pencil ___ I have two _____ and three _____ in my pencil case.   ▶ Check

1

> **Die Personalpronomen**
>
> Personalpronomen ersetzen Nomen (z. B. table → it) oder Eigennamen (z. B. Ben → he).
> Die Personalpronomen sind:
>
> I (ich) we (wir)
> you (du, Sie) you (ihr, Sie)
> he (er) they (sie)
> she (sie)
> it (es)
>
> ❗ Das Pronomen I (ich) wird im Englischen immer **groß**geschrieben.
> Das Pronomen it steht für Dinge und Tiere und entspricht „er", „sie" oder „es":
> *I have a guitar. ~~The guitar~~ It's great.*
> *What page is it?*
>
> ▶ SB p. 24, p. 176

7 My new school

Replace the phrases with *he, she, it, we, they*.
Ersetze die Satzglieder durch he, she, it, we, they.

1 I have a new timetable. ~~The timetable~~ *It* _____ is OK.

2 My class teacher is Ms Ahmed. ~~Ms Ahmed~~ _____ is nice.

3 My friends and I are in the same class. ~~My friends and I~~ _____ are in 7B.

4 Max is a student in my class. ~~Max~~ _____ is from Oxford.

5 Look! Livvy and Dan are very tired. ~~Livvy and Dan~~ _____ are asleep.

8 At school

Match sentences 1–5 with the right sentences A–E. Write the sentences.
Ordne die Sätze 1–5 den Sätzen A–E zu. Schreibe die Sätze.

A ~~She's great.~~
B They're in room 11.
C We're four good friends.
D He's in the classroom.
E It's blue and grey.

Achte in den Sätzen A–E auf die Personalpronomen. Das hilft dir, die richtige Zuordnung zu finden.

1 I like Sunita. – *She's great.*

2 We have a school uniform. – _____

3 Where's Zane? – _____

4 Where are the English lessons? – _____

5 I like Lily, Emma and Tim. – _____

▶ Check

9 Sunita, Lily, Noah and Zane at school

Write the correct words from the box.
Schreibe die richtigen Wörter aus dem Kasten auf.

I • you • he • it • we • they

It's lunch break at Varndean …

Can (1) _____ see Noah and Zane?

No, (2) _____ can't. But (3) _____ know (4) _____ 're here at school.

Oh look, Sunita. Noah is here now.

Oh! Hi, Noah. How are (5) _____ ?

(6) _____ 'm OK, thanks. Can (7) _____ help me with exercise 2 in our English book?

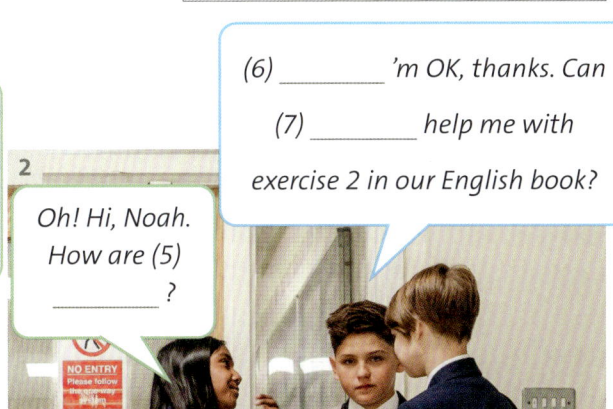

Yes, (8) _____ can. What page is (9) _____ ?

(10) _____ 's page 15.

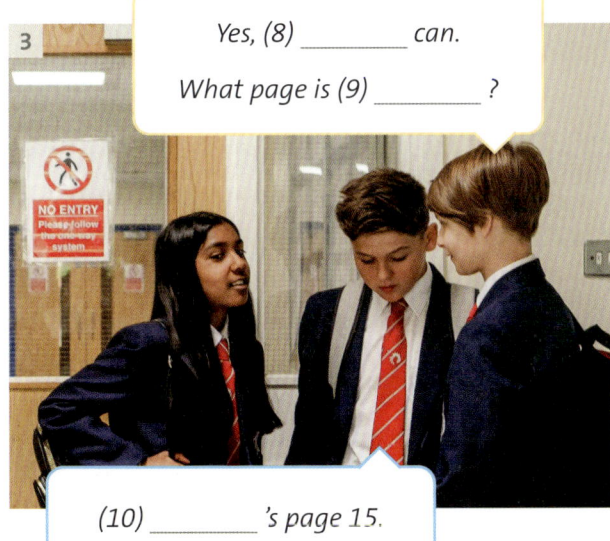

Oh, thanks Lily. And thanks Sunita.

Hey, where's Zane?

(11) _____ think (12) _____ 's with Ms Ahmed.

Hi! Great, (13) _____ 're all here. (14) _____ can play football!

Football? No, (15) _____ 're tired!

► Check

1

Erklärfilm

Das Verb be: Bejahte Aussagesätze

Es gibt zwei Formen von be: Kurzformen (short forms) und Langformen (long forms). Bei den Kurzformen ersetzt ein Apostroph (') einen weggefallenen Buchstaben.

	Langformen	**Kurzformen**	
• bei offiziellen Schreiben	I am	I'm	• beim Sprechen
• nach Eigennamen (Zane, Sunita)	you are	you're	• in persönlichen E-Mails oder Chats
• nach Nomen (bike, teachers)	he is / she is / it is	he's / she's / it's	• nach Pronomen: (I, you, he, she, it, we, you, they)
	we are	we're	
	you are	you're	
	they are	they're	▶ SB p. 24, p. 177

10 Where's Paula?

(Circle) **the right verb forms.** *Kreise die richtigen Verbformen ein.*

1   Hi, we 's / 're Milo and Oliver. What about you?   I 'm / 's Zahra.

2   Where's Paula?   She 'm / 's in the classroom.

3   What about Josh and Tamsin?   They 's / 're in class 7L.

4   Here, you can have my sandwich.   Thank you. I 'm / 're always hungry.

11 Class 7C

Write the correct form: 's or 're. *Schreibe die richtige Verbform: 's oder 're.*

1 We _____ in 7C.

2 My friends? They _____ all in 7K.

3 Look, Ms Khan! She _____ my maths teacher.

4 I like art and PE. They _____ two subjects at my school.

5 Assembly? It _____ on Tuesday and Thursday.

6 Here's my timetable. It _____ OK.

▶ Check

12 Class 7K

Write the sentences in blue in the short form of *be*.
Schreibe die Sätze in Blau in der Kurzform von be.

Mia Is your class OK, Jack?

Jack 1 Yes, I like the students in my class.
They are nice. *They're nice.*

2 We are 25 students in 7K. _____

3 I have a good friend, Olga. She is nice. _____

4 My friend Zack is nice too. He is from London. _____

5 I am happy in my class. _____

Mia Thank you, Jack!

Jack You are welcome, Mia! _____

13 Two messages

a) **Complete the messages with '*m*, '*s* or '*re*.** *Vervollständige die Nachrichten mit 'm, 's oder 're.*

Hi, Nazim. I _____ (1) in London with Dad. It _____ (2) nice here. We _____ (3) in London Zoo. I like the monkeys. They _____ (4) great! ☺ See you soon. Kinga

Hi, Kinga. You _____ (5) lucky. I _____ (6) in Brighton and I can't go swimming with Mum. She _____ (7) tired. And I can't play basketball with Lily and Zane. They _____ (8) busy.

b) **Now write *is* or *are*.** *Schreibe is oder are.*

1 Kinga _____ lucky.

2 She and her dad _____ in London Zoo.

3 It _____ nice there.

4 The monkeys _____ great.

5 But Nazim _____ in Brighton and his mum _____ tired.

6 And Lily and Zane _____ busy.

► Check

1

Erklärfilm

Das Verb *be*: Verneinte Aussagesätze

Bei der Verneinung von *be* benutzt du fast immer die Kurzform.

I **'m not** very big.
You **aren't** very big.
He **isn't** very big.
She **isn't** very big.
It **isn't** very big.
We **aren't** very big.
You **aren't** very big.
They **aren't** very big.

▶ SB p. 29, p. 177

14 Nice or not nice?

(Circle) **the right verb forms.** *Kreise die richtigen Verbformen ein.*

We **isn't / aren't** busy.

Parkour **isn't / aren't** hard.

I **'m not / isn't** lucky!

The cats **'m not / aren't** very happy!

Nav **'m not / isn't** good at yoga.

It **isn't / aren't** great here!

▶ Check

15 At school

Match the sentence parts and write the right letters A–D in the boxes. *Ordne die Satzteile zu und schreibe die richtigen Buchstaben A–D in die Kästchen.*

1 I think geography is great because …   A he isn't at school.

2 I can't go and see Mr Lee now because …   B the students are happy.

3 Liz and Cath aren't my friends because …   C they aren't very nice.

4 It isn't a bad school because …   D it isn't hard.

1 ☐ 2 ☐ 3 ☐ 4 ☐

16 A message from Noah

Complete Noah's message with *'m not* and *aren't*. *Vervollständige Noahs Nachricht mit 'm not und aren't.*

Hi, Sunita,

I'm in a hotel in London. I (1) _____ alone here. I'm here with Mum, Dad and Buddy. We (2) _____ in a very big room, but it's OK. And the food (3) _____ bad. But I (4) _____ happy because you (5) _____ here and because Zane and Lily (6) _____ here.

See you at school.

Noah

▶ Check

> **Der s-Genitiv**
>
> Mit dem s-Genitiv drückst du aus, dass etwas zu jemandem gehört.
>
> | | | |
> |---|---|---|
> | Singular *(Noah, Mr Lee)* | 's | Noah's dog – Noahs Hund |
> | | | Mr Lee's class – Herr Lees Klasse |
> | Plural mit -s *(boys, Watsons)* | s' | the boys' phones – die Handys der Jungen |
> | | | the Watsons' house – das Haus der Watsons |
> | Plural ohne -s *(men, women)* | 's | the men's clothes – die Kleidung der Männer |
> | | | the women's cars – die Autos der Frauen |
>
> ► SB Hello! + Unit 1, p. 174

17 Four sentences and pictures

Write 's or '. Then match the sentences with the pictures A–D. Write the right letter for each sentence.
Schreibe 's oder '. Ordne dann die Sätze den Bildern A–D zu. Schreibe zu jedem Satz den richtigen Buchstaben.

1 Where's Zane ____ tie? ☐

2 This building ____ windows are very small. ☐

3 Those are my friends ____ bikes. ☐

4 I don't like this school ____ uniform. ☐

A

B

C

D

18 An apostrophe – or not?

Look at the <u>underlined</u> words. Put an apostrophe (') in the right place. *Sieh dir die unterstrichenen Wörter an. Setze ein Apostroph (') an die richtige Stelle.*

1 <u>Adams</u> dog is very friendly.

2 <u>My mums</u> favourite colour is pink.

3 <u>The boys</u> name is Tom.

4 <u>The students</u> answers are in the exercise books.

► Check

> **Die *of*-Fügung**
>
> Gehören zwei Sachen zusammen, verbindest du sie mit *of*.
> *the end of the story* – das Ende der Geschichte
>
> *Of* verwendest du auch bei Mengenbezeichnungen.
> *a kilo of oranges* – ein Kilo Orangen
>
> ▶ SB Hello! + Unit 1, p. 174

19 Words that go together

a) **Complete the phrases with the right word from the box. Remember to use the word *of*.**
Vervollständige die Ausdrücke mit dem richtigen Wort aus dem Kasten. Denke an das Wort of.

bag • class • day • ~~map~~ • page

a *map of* Brighton   a _____ *of* apples   a _____ students

a _____ the week   a _____ a book

b) **Read the text. Is the information in the text right or wrong? Tick one box.** *Lies den Text. Sind die Informationen richtig oder falsch? Kreuze an.*

> **Good to know**
>
> **Group words in English**
> In English we say a class of students, a gang of kids and a team of football players. And for a group of fish? We say a school of fish.

I think this information is right ☐ wrong ☐.

▶ Check

20 REVISION A timetable

Look at Lisa's timetable. Circle the right verb forms. *Schau dir Lisas Stundenplan an. Kreise die richtigen Verbformen ein.*

Monday	Tuesday	Wednesday	Thursday	Friday
French	French	geography	English	maths
English	history	maths	maths	French
break	break	break	break	break
science	computing	maths	design and technology	English
science	music	science	history	English
lunch	lunch	lunch	lunch	lunch
computing	art	PE	science	music
design and technology	art	PE	geography	computing

Maths is / isn't on Wednesday, Thursday and Friday.

English is / isn't on Tuesday and Wednesday. It 's / isn't on Monday, Thursday and Friday.

French and computing are / aren't on Monday, Tuesday and Friday. They 're / aren't on Wednesday and Thursday.

Paul   It's Tuesday after lunch. You're in your classroom, right, Lisa?

Lisa   No, I 'm / 'm not in my classroom because I 'm / 'm not in the art room.

21 REVISION Apostrophes

Lisa talks about her school. Look at the underlined words. Put an apostrophe (') in the right place. *Lisa spricht über ihre Schule. Sieh dir die unterstrichenen Wörter an. Setze ein Apostroph (') an die richtige Stelle.*

Vorsicht! Es gibt Apostrophe (') in
- *isn't, aren't, …*
- *my friend's bike, …*

Its Monday today, so were at school. We arent at the beach. This is my classroom.
Oh, Paul and Rufas! Theyre bullies. Theyre mean.
This is my desk and that is my teachers desk.
Oh, this isnt my pen! I think its Bens pen.

► Check

Unit 2
My family and home

Das Verb *be*: Fragen und Kurzantworten

Erklär-film

Bei Fragen steht *be* am Anfang des Satzes.
You *are* English. → *Are* you English?   She *is* brave. → *Is* she brave?

Antworte auf eine Frage nicht einfach mit *yes* oder *no*. Das klingt unhöflich. Verwende Kurzantworten.

Fragen	Kurzantworten
Am I right?	Yes, you are. / No, you aren't.
Are you tired?	Yes, I am. / No, I'm not.
	Yes, we are. / No, we aren't.
Is Freya nice?	Yes, she is. / No, she isn't.
Is it late?	Yes, it is. / No, it isn't.
Are Tim and Lisa happy?	Yes, they are. / No, they aren't.

▶ SB p. 47, p. 178

1 Questions and answers at school

a) (Circle) the correct form in the questions. *Kreise in den Fragen die richtige Form ein.*

1 Sorry, Sir. Am / Are I late for school?   No, _____.

2 Are / Is it Monday today?   Yes, _____.

3 Am / Are you OK, Zane?   No, _____.

4 Are / Is we in room 9 today?   Yes, _____.

5 Are / Is Lily and Noah at school today?   No, _____.

b) Now complete the answers with the right phrases from the box. *Vervollständige nun die Antworten mit den richtigen Ausdrücken aus dem Kasten.*

I'm not • it is • they aren't • we are • you aren't

seventeen 17

2 A phone call from Mum

Meg's mum phones Meg. Complete her questions with *Is* or *Are*. Then look at the pictures and write short answers.
Megs Mutter ruft Meg an. Vervollständige ihre Fragen mit Is oder Are. Schau dir dann die Bilder an und schreibe Kurzantworten.

Is he OK?
— Yes, he is. / No, he isn't.
Is she OK?
— Yes, she is. / No, she isn't.
Are they OK?
— Yes, they are. / No, they aren't.

1 _____ you at home, Meg?
Yes, I _____

2 _____ your room messy?
No, it _____

3 _____ your sister happy?
_____

4 _____ your brothers quiet?
_____

5 _____ Dad angry?
_____

6 And I think you are tired, Meg. _____ I right?
Yes, you _____

3 Tibbs, my cat

Complete the questions and the short answers. *Vervollständige die Fragen und die Kurzantworten.*

Where *is* _____ Tibbs?

_____ she under my bed? No, she _____.

Tibbs, where _____ you?

_____ she with our neighbour's cat Moggy? _____ Tibbs and Moggy in the garden? No, they _____.

Tibbs, I'm angry with you!

_____ I angry with Tibbs? No, I _____. I can't be angry with Tibbs.

4 Questions and answers

Match the questions 1–5 with the answers A–E.
Ordne die Fragen 1–5 den Antworten A–E zu.

1 Where is your house?
2 Who are your neighbours?
3 What is under the table?
4 Who is your class teacher?
5 What are your favourite colours?

A Yellow and green.
B Ms Patel.
C In Edmund Road.
D Mike and Rowena.
E My cat.

> Das Fragewort steht vor am / is / are.
> *Where* am I? – Wo bin ich?
> *Who* are you? – Wer bist du?

> **There is ... / There are ...**
>
> Mit *there is* (*there's*) und *there are* sagst du, dass etwas vorhanden ist. Im Deutschen heißt es meist: Es gibt ..., Da sind ..., Es stehen ..., Da liegen ...
>
> Du verwendest:
> - *There's* ... mit dem Singular
>   *There's a cat in our kitchen.* – *Da ist eine Katze in unserer Küche.*
>   *Is there a toilet here? – Yes, there is.* – *Gibt es hier eine Toilette? – Ja.*
>
> - *There are* ... mit dem Plural
>   *There are three bedrooms in our flat.* – *Es gibt drei Schlafzimmer in unserer Wohnung.*
>   *Are there lots of people here? – Yes, there are.* – *Gibt es hier viele Menschen? – Ja.*
>
> ▶ SB p. 50, p. 178

5 What's in the garden?

a) **Complete the sentences with *There's* or *There are*.** *Vervollständige die Sätze mit* There's *oder* There are.

1. _____ two nice big trees in the garden.
2. _____ four people in the garden: two boys and two girls.
3. _____ two animals: two cats.
4. _____ a brown table.
5. _____ a black and white football.
6. _____ a yellow bike.

b) **Complete the questions. Then look at the picture and complete the answers.** *Vervollständige die Fragen. Sieh dir dann das Bild an und vervollständige die Antworten.*

1. *Is* _____ there a cat in the garden? Yes, there *is* _____ .
2. _____ there some chairs in the garden? Yes, there _____ .
3. _____ there a lot of rabbits in the garden? No, _____ .
4. _____ there a hamster in the garden? No, _____ .

Die Possessivbegleiter

Possessivbegleiter zeigen an, wem etwas gehört.

I	→	*my* sister – meine Schwester	we	→	*our* kitchen – unsere Küche
you	→	*your* house – dein Haus	you	→	*your* car – euer Auto
he	→	*his* clothes – seine Kleider	they	→	*their* bedroom – ihr Schlafzimmer
she	→	*her* laptop – ihr Laptop			
it	→	*its* colour – seine/ihre Farbe			

!

- *it's* = *it is*: *It's cold today.* – *Es ist kalt heute.*
  its = sein, ihr: *our garden with its trees* – *unser Garten mit seinen Bäumen*

- *they're* = *they are*: *They're German.* – *Sie sind Deutsche.*
  Their = ihr(e): *Here are Dan and Jo with their dad.* – *Hier sind Dan und Jo mit ihrem Vater.*

▶ SB Units 1–2, p. 176

---

6 Photos

Sunita shows Noah some photos. Circle the correct words. *Sunita zeigt Noah Fotos. Kreise die richtigen Wörter ein.*

1. Look! That's my / our brother and our / her parrot George.
2. And that's me in my / their room.
3. And there are my / his mum and Ben in our / their bedroom.
4. There's Willow with her / his new phone.
5. And that's you, Noah, with your / her dog!

---

7 Sunita's family

Complete the sentences with the words from the box.
Vervollständige die Sätze mit den Wörtern aus dem Kasten.

> her • my • our • their • ~~your~~

Noah Is all (1) *your* _____ family in Brighton, Sunita?

Sunita Well, Mum, Nish and I are in Brighton. (2) _____ house is in Palmeira Road. Mum is a vet and there are animals from (3) _____ work in our house. And there are Ben and Willow. (4) _____ house is in Brighton too. But Aunt Priya, Uncle Rahi, Jay and Neeta live in Birmingham. Jay and Neeta are (5) _____ cousins.

8 At Sunita's house

Noah is at Sunita's house. Complete his sentences with *it's* or *its*.
Noah ist in Sunitas Haus. Vervollständige seine Sätze mit it's *oder* its.

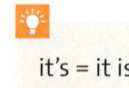

it's = it is

I really like your house with (1) _____ nice big garden.
There are a lot of trees here. (2) _____ nice.
Wow! And I like your room! (3) _____ really cool. And I like your sofa with (4) _____ nice cushions! I like your parrot and I like (5) _____ name too.
Oh look, (6) _____ late. Time to go home.

9 REVISION Khaled's new house

(Circle) the correct words. *Kreise die richtigen Wörter ein.*

Dan Are you in your / his new house, Khaled?

Khaled Yes, Dan, I am / are.

Dan And are / is it nice?

Khaled Yes, it is. Its / It's really nice. I have our / my own room with a bed, of course, a wardrobe and a desk. Oh, and some shelves.

Dan And what about your neighbours. Is / Are they nice?

Khaled Yes, he / they are. And there are / their dog is really cute.

Her / My name is Melanie. You must come and see me here, Dan!

Unit 3
My day

Das simple present

Mit dem *simple present* sagst du, was oft, jeden Tag oder nie passiert.

I / you / we / they play
he / she/ it / my sister plays   ❗ *He, she* und *it*, das *-s* muss mit!

Häufige Signalwörter im *simple present* sind: *always* (immer), *often* (oft), *sometimes* (manchmal), *never* (nie).

▶ SB p. 80, p.179

1 Sunita's school day

a) Read Sunita's text. <u>Underline</u> the signal words for the simple present. *Lies Sunitas Text. Unterstreiche die Signalwörter für das simple present.*

b) Highlight the verbs that end in *-s*. *Markiere die Verben, die auf -s enden.*

I always get up at 6.15. School starts at 8.45. I get the bus at 8.15, or my mum sometimes takes me by car.

I like science, but I often find art quite hard. I never draw nice pictures. But Lily often draws very cool pictures.

I never come home for lunch – I always eat at school.

School ends at 2.55 and I come home by bus.

We have dinner at six o'clock and I often go to bed before nine o'clock.

2 Sunita and Willow

Read Sunita's sentences. Then complete the sentences about Willow. Use the verbs in blue.
Lies Sunitas Sätze. Vervollständige dann die Sätze über Willow. Verwende die Verben in Blau.

1 I get up at 6.15.   A Willow _____ up at 7.00.

2 I like science.   B Willow _____ maths.

3 I find art quite hard.   C She _____ English quite hard.

4 I always eat at school.   D She always _____ at school too.

▶ Check

3 Crossword

a) **Look at the pictures. Write the verbs from the box.** *Schau dir die Bilder an. Schreibe die Verben aus dem Kasten auf.*

cooks • listens • phone • plays • walks • write

My friend Jason ... to music.

My dad ... on Sundays.

My friends Dan and Eli ... stories.

I often ... my friends.

My mum ... to her work.

My sister ... the guitar.

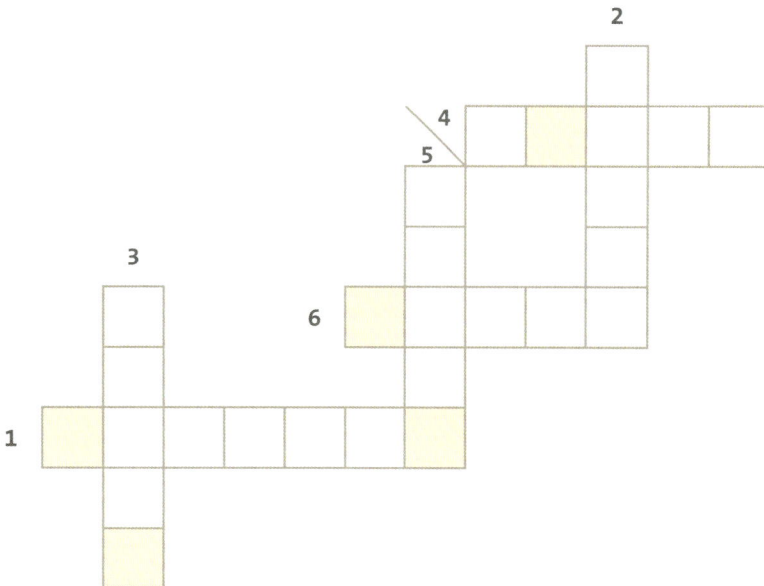

b) **The highlighted letters in 3a) make a word. Write it.**
Die markierten Buchstaben in 3a) ergeben ein Wort. Schreibe es.

Zane always _____ his mum at home.   ▶ Check

4 My brother Isaac

Add -s to the verbs if necessary. *Ergänze -s am Ende des Verbs, wo nötig.*

I love____ my brother Isaac. He's only four years old, but he love____ books. I often read____ to him when I come____ home from school. He really like____ that and he often ask____ a lot of questions. He often draw____ pictures or dream____ when I read____ to him. Then we often talk____ about the book. And he remember____ all about the story!

5 My week

Write sentences in the simple present. *Schreibe Sätze im simple present.*

1 On Mondays – I – always – play football
   On Mondays I always play football.

2 On Tuesdays – my sister – often – go swimming
   On Tuesdays my sister often

3 On Wednesdays – Dad – never – come home – before 8 p.m.
   On Wednesdays Dad

4 On Thursdays – Mum – often – go – to yoga

5 On Fridays – we – always – eat fish – for dinner

▶ Check

3

> **Das simple present: Sonderformen**
>
> Es gibt im *simple present* ein paar Sonderformen bei *he/she/it*:
>
> - -ss, -x, -sh, -ch oder -o + -es:
>   brush: He bru**s**h**es** his teeth.   go: She go**es** to school.
>   watch: My sister wat**ch**es TV.   do: My dad d**o**es parkour.
>
> - Konsonant (b, c, d, ... z) + y wird zu -ies: tidy: My brother ti**d**ies his room.
>
> - have → has: Our flat has three bedrooms.
>
> ▶ SB p. 80, p. 179

6 Students in Toyin's class

Match the sentences. Write the right letters A–D in the boxes. *Ordne die Sätze zu. Schreibe die richtigen Buchstaben A–D in die Kästchen.*

1 Leo isn't messy.   A He brushes it every day.

2 Ravi has a nice dog.   B He always tidies his desk after the lesson.

3 Tim isn't nice.   C She watches all the big rugby matches on TV.

4 Emma is a rugby fan.   D He often bullies other student at school.

1 ☐   2 ☐   3 ☐   4 ☐

7 Toyin and her sister

Write the verbs in the simple present. *Schreibe die Verben im simple present.*

My sister and I _____ (1 have) very different hobbies.

I'm a football fan and I _____ (2 play) in a club in town. My sister sometimes _____ (3 come) to the club too and _____ (4 watch) us.

My sister _____ (5 have) dancing lessons. She always _____ (6 go) to her dancing lesson on Tuesdays. She _____ (7 do) some really nice dancing moves!

▶ Check

Die Wortstellung

In Aussagesätzen ist die Wortstellung: subject – verb – object.

Dad	makes	dinner	when	he	comes	home from work
Papa	macht	das Abendessen,	wenn	er	von der Arbeit nach Hause	kommt.

Mit Häufigkeitsadverbien (*always, often, sometimes, never*) kannst du sagen, wie oft etwas geschieht. Anders als im Deutschen stehen sie im Englischen meist direkt vor dem Hauptverb.
We sometimes play a game. – Wir spielen manchmal ein Spiel.

▶ SB p. 83, p. 179

8 The right order

Write the right word in each line. *Schreibe das richtige Wort in jede Zeile.*

always • never • often • sometimes

 1 _____

 2 _____

 3 _____

4 _____

9 Cooking club

Write the words in the right order. *Schreibe die Wörter in der richtigen Reihenfolge.*

1 always / meet

We _always_ _____ on Wednesday after school.

2 meet / sometimes

And we _____ _____ on Saturday morning.

3 cook / often

We _____ _____ nice food.

4 never / have

We _____ _____ a bad time.

▶ Check

3

10 What are their hobbies?

Find the hobbies. Write sentences. *Finde die Hobbys. Schreibe Sätze.*

1 I always — plays table tennis.
2 Olivia sometimes — go windsurfing.
3 My brother never — goes running.
4 Paula often — does dancing.

_____
_____
_____
_____

11 You're the teacher!

Here's an article about sport in German schools. But there are five mistakes in it. First correct the article with arrows. Then complete the corrected text. *Hier ist ein Artikel über Sport an deutschen Schulen. Allerdings haben sich fünf Fehler eingeschlichen. Markiere zuerst die Fehler mit Pfeilen. Vervollständige dann den korrigierten Text.*

Sport in German schools

In German schools we play never cricket. We play often handball and basketball. We play often football in clubs in town and not at school. But I think schools in Germany have always a sports hall.

In German schools _____
_____
_____ and basketball.
_____
_____
_____
and not at school. But I think _____
_____
_____

▶ Check

28 twenty-eight

Basic lighthouse 1

Grammarmaster

Lösungen

Lösungen

Unit 1 My new school

1 T-shirts
a)
1. **a** lion
2. **a** horse
3. **an** elephant
4. **a** seagull
5. **an** apple
6. **an** orange
7. **a** hat
8. **a** bike

b)
1. **A** horse is **an** animal.
2. You can eat **an** apple.
3. I can see **a** zebra, **a** gorilla and **an** orang utan.

> Alle Lösungen aus diesem Heft findest du auch in deiner Cornelsen Lernen App.

2 At school
a) b)
1. I have a **b**ook. It's a **b**ig book. It's an **E**nglish book.
2. And I have a **p**encil. It's an **o**ld pencil, but I like it.
3. I have an **e**xercise book. It's an **o**range exercise book.

3 Mr Lee's sentences
a) b)

	ðə	ði
1 Look at the **b**oard!	✓	
2 Open the **b**ook at page 21.	✓	
3 Eat the **a**pple, please.		✓
4 Listen to the **E**nglish students.		✓

4 Sunita is at the zoo
I can see two **elephants**, three **men**, four **women**, five **snakes**, six **lions**, seven **children** and eight **parrots**.

5 Words with -y
a) b)
1. holid**a**y – holidays
2. hob**b**y – hobbies
3. monk**e**y – monkeys
4. po**n**y – ponies

6 More than one
a) b)
1. friend: **1** – Hassan and Sasha are my **friends**.
2. baby: **3** – I love **babies**.
3. box: **2** – Look at the words in the two **boxes**.
4. sandwich: **2** – I eat **sandwiches** at school.
5. pen, pencil: **1** – I have two **pens** and three **pencils** in my pencil case.

7 My new school
1 I have a new timetable. **It** is OK.
2 My class teacher is Ms Ahmed. **She** is nice.
3 My friends and I are in the same class. **We** are in 7B.
4 Max is a student in my class. **He** is from Oxford.
5 Look! Livvy and Dan are very tired. **They** are asleep.

8 At school
1 She's great.
2 It's blue and grey.
3 He's in the classroom.
4 They're in room 11.
5 We're four good friends.

9 Sunita, Lily, Noah and Zane at school
1 you • 2 I • 3 I • 4 they • 5 you • 6 I • 7 you • 8 I / we • 9 it • 10 It • 11 I • 12 he • 13 you / we • 14 We • 15 we

10 Where's Paula?
1 Hi, we**'re** Milo and Oliver. What about you? – I**'m** Zahra.
2 Where's Paula? – She**'s** in the classroom.
3 What about Josh and Tamsin? – They**'re** in class 7L.
4 Here, you can have my sandwich. – Thank you. I**'m** always hungry.

11 Class 7C
1 We**'re** in 7C.
2 My friends? They**'re** all in 7K.
3 Look, Ms Khan! She**'s** my maths teacher.
4 I like art and PE. They**'re** two subjects at my school.
5 Assembly? It**'s** on Tuesday and Thursday.
6 Here's my timetable. It**'s** OK.

12 Class 7K
1 They're nice.
2 We're 25 students in 7K.
3 She's nice.
4 He's from London.
5 I'm happy in my class.
6 You're welcome, Mia!

Lösungen

13 Two messages
a)
Hi Nazim. I'm in London with Dad. It's nice here. We're in London Zoo. I like the monkeys. They're great! See you soon. Kinga
Hi, Kinga. You're lucky. I'm in Brighton and I can't go swimming with Mum. She's tired. And I can't play basketball with Lily and Zane. They're busy.

b)
1. Kinga **is** lucky.
2. She and her dad **are** in London Zoo.
3. It **is** nice there.
4. The monkeys **are** great.
5. But Nazim **is** in Brighton and his mum **is** tired.
6. And Lily and Zane **are** busy.

14 Nice or not nice?
1. We **aren't** busy.
2. Parkour **isn't** hard.
3. I'**m not** lucky!
4. The cats **aren't** very happy!
5. Nav **isn't** good at yoga.
6. It **isn't** great here!

15 At school
1 D • 2 A • 3 C • 4 B

16 A message from Noah
Hi, Sunita, I'm in a hotel in London. I'**m not** alone here. I'm here with Mum, Dad and Buddy. We **aren't** in a very big room, but it's OK. And the food **isn't** bad. But I'**m not** happy because you **aren't** here and because Zane and Lily **aren't** here. See you at school. Noah

17 Four sentences and pictures
1. Where's Zane's tie? C
2. This building's windows are very small. B
3. Those are my friends' bikes. D
4. I don't like this school's uniform. A

18 An apostrophe – or not?
1. Adam's dog is very friendly.
2. My mum's favourite colour is pink.
3. The boy's name is Tom.
4. The students' answers are in the exercise books.

19 Words that go together
a)
1. a map of Brighton
2. a bag of apples
3. a class of students
4. a day of the week
5. a page of a book

b)
The information is right.

20 REVISION **A timetable**

Maths **is** on Wednesday, Thursday and Friday.
English **isn't** on Tuesday and Wednesday. It**'s** on Monday, Thursday and Friday.
French and computing **are** on Monday, Tuesday and Friday. They **aren't** on Wednesday and Thursday.
Paul It's Tuesday after lunch. You're in your classroom, right, Lisa?
Lisa No, I**'m** not in my classroom because I**'m** in the art room.

✉ 21 REVISION **Apostrophes**

It's Monday today, so we're at school. We aren't at the beach. This is my classroom.
Oh, Paul and Rufas! They're bullies. They're mean.
This is my desk and that is my class teacher's desk.
Oh, this isn't my pen! I think it's Ben's pen.

Unit 2 My family and home

1 Questions and answers at school
a) b)
1 Sorry, Sir. **Am** I late for school? – No, **you aren't**.
2 **Is** it Monday today? – Yes, **it is**.
3 **Are** you OK, Zane? – No, **I'm not**.
4 **Are** we in room 9 today? – Yes, **we are**.
5 **Are** Lily and Noah at school today? – No, **they aren't**.

2 A phone call from Mum
1 **Are** you at home, Meg? – **Yes, I am**.
2 **Is** your room messy? – **No, it isn't**.
3 **Is** your sister happy? – **Yes, she is**.
4 **Are** your brothers quiet? – **No, they aren't**.
5 **Is** Dad angry? – **Yes, he is**.
6 And I think you are tired, Meg. **Am** I right? – **Yes, you are**.

3 Tibbs, my cat
1 Where **is** Tibbs?
2 **Is** she under my bed? No, she **isn't**.
3 Tibbs, where **are** you?
4 **Is** she with our neighbour's cat Moggy. **Are** Tibbs and Moggy in the garden? No, they **aren't**.
6 **Am** I angry with Tibbs? No, I**'m not**. I can't be angry with Tibbs.

4 Questions and answers
1 C • 2 D • 3 E • 4 B • 5 A

Lösungen

5 What's in the garden?
a)
1. **There are** two nice big trees in the garden.
2. **There are** four people in the garden: two boys and two girls.
3. **There are** two animals: two cats.
4. **There's** a brown table.
5. **There's** a black and white football.
6. **There's** a yellow bike.

b)
1. **Is** there a cat in the garden? Yes, there **is**.
2. **Are** there some chairs in the garden? Yes, there **are**.
3. **Are** there a lot of rabbits in the garden? No, **there aren't**.
4. **Is** there a hamster in the garden? No, **there isn't**.

6 Photos
1. Look! That's **my** brother and **our** parrot George.
2. And that's me in **my** room.
3. And there are **my** mum and Ben in **their** bedroom.
4. There's Willow with **her** new phone.
5. And that's you, Noah, with **your** dog!

7 Sunita's family
1. your
2. Our
3. her
4. Their
5. my

8 At Sunita's house
1. its
2. It's
3. It's
4. its
5. its
6. it's

9 REVISION Khaled's new house

Dan   Are you in **your** new house, Khaled?
Khaled   Yes, Dan, I **am**.
Dan   And **is** it nice?
Khaled   Yes, it is. **It's** really nice. I have **my** own room with a bed, of course, a wardrobe and a desk. Oh, and some shelves.
Dan   And what about your neighbours. **Are** they nice?
Khaled   Yes, **they** are. And **their** dog is really cute. **Her** name is Melanie. You must come and see me here, Dan!

Unit 3 My day

1 Sunita's school day
a) b)
I <u>always</u> get up at 6.15. School starts at 8.45. I get the bus at 8.15, or my mum <u>sometimes</u> takes me by car.
I like science, but I <u>often</u> find art quite hard. I <u>never</u> draw nice pictures.
But Lily <u>often</u> draws very cool pictures.
I <u>never</u> come home for lunch – I <u>always</u> eat at school.
School ends at 2.55 and I come home by bus.
We have dinner at six o'clock and I <u>often</u> go to bed before nine o'clock.

2 Sunita and Willow
A Willow **gets up** at 7.00.
B Willow **likes** maths.
C She **finds** English quite hard.
D She always **eats** at school too.

3 Crossword
a)

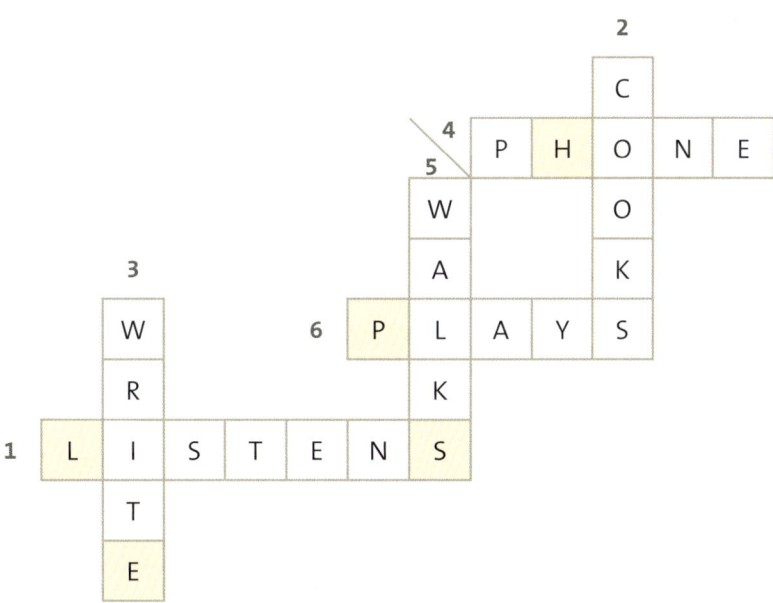

b)
Zane always **helps** his mum at home.

4 My brother Isaac
I love my brother Isaac. He's only four years old, but he love**s** books. I often read to him when I come home from school. He really like**s** that and he often ask**s** a lot of questions. He often draw**s** pictures or dream**s** when I read to him. Then we often talk about the book. And he remember**s** all about the story!

5 My week
1 On Mondays I always play football.
2 On Tuesdays my sister often goes swimming.
3 On Wednesdays Dad never comes home before 8 p.m.
4 On Thursdays Mum often goes to yoga.
5 On Fridays we always eat fish for dinner.

Lösungen

6 Students in Toyin's class
1 B • 2 A • 3 D • 4 C

7 Toyin and her sister
My sister and I **have** very different hobbies.
I'm a football fan and I **play** in a club in town. My sister sometimes **comes** to the club too and **watches** us. My sister **has** dancing lessons. She always **goes** to her dancing lesson on Tuesdays. She **does** some really nice dancing moves!

8 The right order
1 always
2 often
3 sometimes
4 never

9 Cooking club
1 We **always meet** on Wednesday after school.
2 And we **sometimes meet** on Saturday morning.
3 We **often cook** nice food.
4 We **never have** a bad time.

10 What are their hobbies?
1 I always go windsurfing.
2 Olivia sometimes goes running.
3 My brother never does dancing.
4 Paula often plays table tennis.

11 You're the teacher!
In German schools we **never play** cricket. We **often play** handball and basketball. We **often play** football in clubs in town and not at school. But I think schools in Germany **always have** a sports hall.

12 REVISION Quiz: Who is it?
a)
1 He cook**s** food for his family. He**'s** a good swimmer. His mum use**s** a wheelchair. He take**s** Holly to her school.	Zane
2 She goe**s** to school by bus. She like**s** computers and she often doe**s** coding. She help**s** Noah when Jade bull**ies** him.	Sunita
3 This boy goe**s** to school by car. He like**s** his dog. He**'s** always hungry.	Noah

b)
4 She often does parkour.	Lily
5 He's often tired because **he always works long days in a cafe.**	Eno / Zane's dad

Unit 4 Where I live

1 East Dean

a)
I live in East Dean. It's a small village and it **doesn't have** big estates. It **isn't** next to the sea, so it **doesn't have** a pier or a marina. And it **doesn't have** a cinema. The children of East Dean **don't go** to school there: they go to school in Eastbourne. My parents **don't work** there because they work in Eastbourne too. My brother and sister **don't like** East Dean because it **doesn't have** a sports centre. But I like East Dean because it's my home.

b)
1 I **don't** watch films in East Dean because it **doesn't** have a cinema.
2 Young people **don't** go to school in East Dean because it **doesn't** have a secondary school.
3 East Dean **doesn't** have many places and my parents **don't** work there.
4 East Dean **doesn't** have rubbish in its streets. Why? I **don't** know why.

2 The lost bag
1 don't
2 don't
3 doesn't
4 don't
5 doesn't
6 don't
7 don't
8 doesn't

3 Zane and Noah are different
1 Zane gets up at 7 a.m., but Noah doesn't **get up** at 7 a.m.
2 Zane walks to school, but Noah doesn't **walk** to school.
3 Zane has a sister, Holly, but Noah doesn't **have** a sister.
4 Zane takes Holly to school, but Noah doesn't **take** Holly to school.
5 Zane goes swimming, but Noah doesn't **go** swimming.
6 Zane watches TV, but Noah doesn't **watch** TV.

4 Some students in my class
1 Radhia and Diya **don't live** on my estate.
2 Kiera **doesn't go** to the youth centre.
3 Max **reads** a book.
4 Cindy **doesn't cook** for her family.
5 Luca **does** skateboarding.

5 Zara's new flat
1 have
2 have
3 share
4 walk
5 use
6 watches
7 come
8 say
9 thinks

6 Likes and dislikes
1. I don't have a dog.
2. She doesn't play table tennis.
3. We don't live in a house.
4. My parents like fish and chips. They don't like soup.
5. Mum does yoga. She doesn't do parkour.
6. Our neighbour has a bike. He doesn't have a car.

7 Questions for you
1. Yes, I do. / No, I don't.
2. Yes, it does. / No, it doesn't.
3. Yes, I do. / No, I don't.
4. Yes, it does. / No, it doesn't.

8 Questions about Lily
1. **Do** Lily and her parents live on an estate? – Yes, they do.
2. **Does** Lily's estate have some problems? – Yes, it does.
3. **Does** Lily live with her sister? – No, she doesn't.
4. **Do** Lily and her parents have friendly neighbours? – Yes, they do.
5. **Does** Lily's dad sometimes walk in the park with Lily? – Yes, he does.

9 Saturday activities
a) b)
1. **Does** Grace go to the pier on Saturdays? – **Yes, she does.**
2. **Do** Sam and Jo go shopping in the Lanes on Saturdays? – **Yes, they do.**
3. **Do** Mr and Mrs Jones go to Jubilee Library on Saturdays? – **No, they don't.**
4. **Does** Milan go to the Brighton i360 on Saturdays? – **Yes, he does.**
5. **Does** Hannah go to St. Nicholas Rest Garden on Saturdays? – **No, she doesn't.**
6. **Do** Phil and his friends go to the station on Saturdays? – **No, they don't.**
7. **Does** Norah go to the museum on Saturdays? – **Yes, she does.**
8. **Do** Amy and her dad go to the shopping centre on Saturdays? – **Yes, they do.**

10 Questions about school
1. How **do** you go to school? – By bus.
2. When **does** your first lesson start? – At 8.50 a.m.
3. Where **do** you have lunch? – In the canteen.
4. What **do** you do in your lunch break? – I talk with my friends.

11 More questions about school
1. ✓
2. ✓
3. When **does** your sister go to school?
4. What **do** you have for lunch?
5. ✓
6. How **do** Zane and Holly get to school?

12 REVISION Brighton beach

I love a summer's day on the beach. Everybody look**s** happy! We bring a picnic and sit on the beach. Mum always go**es** swimming, but Dad **doesn't** swim when it's cold. Then Mum read**s** a book and Dad do**es** a crossword. I listen to music. In the afternoon we often go to the pier and Dad buys rock. The pier close**s** at 6 p.m., but we often **don't** want to go home then.

13 REVISION At Hove Skatepark
1. I **don't** like skateboarding.
2. I **can't** skateboard very well.
3. Skateboarding **isn't** fun!
4. My skateboard **doesn't** work well!

14 REVISION Weekends

Zane What **do** you do at the weekend?
Lily I **don't** know. Mum often **doesn't** want to go out. She **wants** to stay at home. But I sometimes **go** out with Dad. And I often **go** to the youth centre. What **do** you do at the weekend, Zane?
Zane I often **cook** for my family. They all **like** that. **Do** you cook in your family?
Lily No, I **don't**.

15 REVISION Too many questions about the pier

Tourist **Is it** free to go on the pier?
Zane Yes, it is.
Tourist **Are there** trampolines?
Zane Yes, there are.
Tourist **Do they** have special activities at Halloween?
Zane Yes, they do. They have special activities at Halloween and also at Christmas.
Tourist **Can you** buy fish and chips on the pier?
Zane Yes, you can.
Tourist And when **does it** close?
Zane It closes at 6 p.m.
Tourist Thank you. But it's cloudy and windy. I think it's too cold for the pier today!

Unit 5 Enjoy!

1 Noah's visit to London Zoo
a)
1. I**'m** taking lots of photos today.
2. Listen to the parrots! They**'re** making a lot of noise!
3. Look! That big tiger! It**'s** watching me!
4. And the visitors? They**'re** enjoying the sun.

b)
1. 'm visiting
2. 're walking
3. 're standing
4. 's eating
5. 'm (really) enjoying

Lösungen

2 Three activities
1 Look! Jody and Mark **are making** a cake! They**'re putting** strawberries on it.
2 Jo **is looking** happy. She**'s smiling** because her mum **is making** her birthday cake.
3 I**'m eating** an Indian dish, matter paneer. And my friend Kabir **is writing** the recipe for me.

3 Double letters
1 run**n**ing
2 win**n**ing
3 swim**m**ing
4 sit**t**ing
5 stop**p**ing
6 get**t**ing

4 Meera and Ben are away one weekend
a)
1 Sunita and Nish aren't **cleaning the kitchen.**
2 The dishwasher **isn't working.**
3 I'm so worried about Sunita and Nish that I**'m not sleeping.**

b)
1 are enjoying
2 'm not getting up
3 'm not doing
4 isn't taking
5 are eating
6 aren't making
7 isn't working

5 What are you doing?
((Individuelle Lösungen))

6 What are they doing?
1 Are you doing your homework? – Yes, I am.
2 Is Dad doing the shopping at the moment? – No, he isn't.
3 Are you and Hamza making lunch today? – No, we aren't.
4 Are Noah and Zane talking? – Yes, they are.
5 Is Sunita eating breakfast now? – Yes, she is.

7 A birthday party
a)
1 **Are** the girls **having** a birthday party? – Yes, they **are**.
2 **Is** it **raining**? – **No, it isn't.**
3 **Are** the girls **smiling**? – **Yes, they are.**
4 **Are** they **wearing** birthday hats? – **No, they aren't.**
5 **Are** the girls **singing**? – **No, they aren't.**
6 **Is** one girl **eating**? – **Yes, it is.**

b)
1 is having
2 is (she) doing
3 are dancing
4 is (Helena) dancing
5 isn't dancing
6 's eating
7 's watching
8 's smiling
9 is playing
10 are having

8 Much or many?
a)
1 P • 2 P • 3 S • 4 P • 5 S • 6 P • 7 S • 8 S
b)

How much …?	How many …?
flour	bikes
money	ballons
love	men
time	people

9 Questions about school
1 By bus. But there aren't **many** buses from our estate to town. So I usually stand.
2 The food isn't bad, but I think the problem is that we don't get **much** time to eat it.
3 It's OK. We often don't get **much** homework. That's good.
4 Yes, it is. I think we don't do **much** sport at school.
5 Usually yes. But I think it's maybe hard for students who don't have **many** friends.

10 Quiz
1 How **many** players are there in a rugby team?   B fifteen
2 How **much** food does an elephant eat in a day?   B 150 to 160 kilos
3 How **much** rain does London get?   A about the same as Paris
4 How **many** colours does a rainbow have?   B seven
5 How **many** people live in Britain?   A over 65 million
6 How **much** time can a game of cricket take?   B three to five days

11 Lily and Zane's picnic
a) b)
1 Zane   How **many** eggs do we have?
   Lily   There aren't **many eggs.**
2 Zane   How **much** ham do we have?
   Lily   There isn't **much ham.**
3 Zane   How **many** carrots do we have?
   Lily   There aren't **many carrots.**
4 Zane   How **many** sausages do we have?
   Lily   There aren't **many sausages.**

Lösungen

12 REVISION Verbs

help → helping	write → writing	get → getting
go → going	make → making	swim → swimming
buy → buying	take → taking	stop → stopping
look → looking	give → giving	run → running
enjoy → enjoying	dance → dancing	sit → sitting

13 REVISION What are you doing, Noah?

1 What **are** you **doing**, Noah? – I'm going to Lily's birthday party.
2 Who **is going** with you? – Buddy is going with me.
3 What **are** you **taking** in your bag? – A present for Lily, Buddy's favourite ball, my phone, …

15 REVISION And you?

a)
((Individuelle Lösungen))
b)
((Lösungsbeispiel))
I'm writing sentences.
I'm not phoning my friends.
My mum is working in the garden.
My dad isn't helping my mum.

42 forty-two

Lösungen

12 REVISION Quiz: Who is it?

a) **Complete the sentences with -s, -es, -'s or -ies. Then write who it is.** *Vervollständige die Sätze mit -s, -es, -'s oder -ies. Schreibe dann den Namen der gesuchten Person.*

1 He cook _____ food for his family. He _____ a good swimmer. His mum use _____ a wheelchair. He take _____ Holly to her school.

2 She go _____ to school by bus. She like _____ computers and she often do _____ coding. She help _____ Noah when Jade bull _____ him.

3 This boy go _____ to school by car. He like _____ his dog. He _____ always hungry.

b) **Write sentences. Put the words in the right order. Then write who it is.** *Schreibe Sätze. Bringe die Wörter in die richtige Reihenfolge. Schreibe dann den Namen der gesuchten Person.*

4 often / parkour / does / she

She _____

5 long days in a cafe / always / works / he

He's often tired because *he* _____

_____

▶ Check

Unit 4
Where I live

Das simple present: Verneinte Aussagesätze

Um Aussagen im *simple present* zu verneinen, verwendest du don't oder doesn't.

| I, you, we, they, my parents | + don't + verb | he, she, it, my brother | + doesn't + verb |

I don't like maths. – Ich mag Mathe nicht.
My mum doesn't work in town. – Meine Mutter arbeitet nicht in der Stadt.
We don't play cricket. – Wir spielen nicht Cricket.

▶ SB p. 107, p. 180

1 East Dean

a) **Oscar writes about his village. Read his text. Highlight the verbs in the negative.** *Oscar schreibt über sein Dorf. Lies seinen Text. Markiere alle verneinten Verben.*

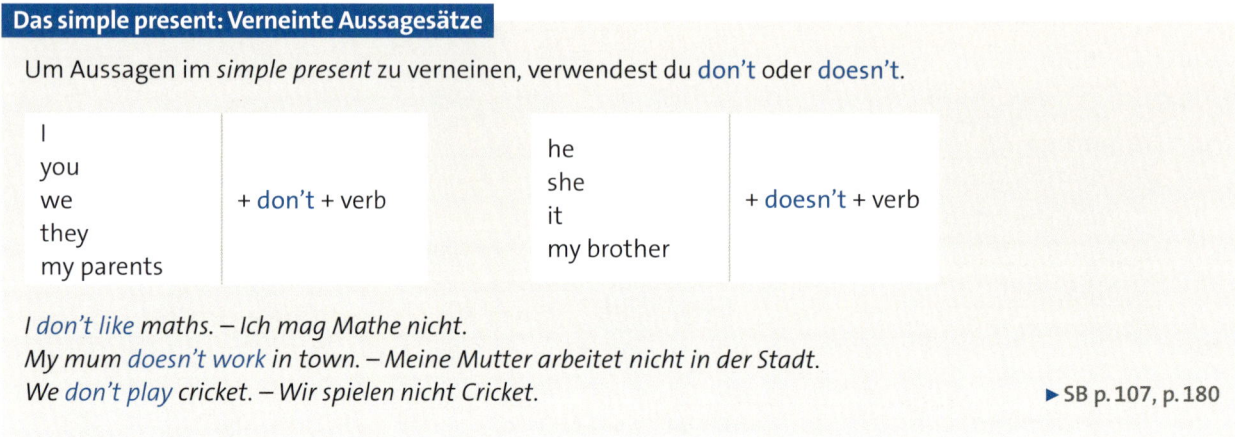

www.eastdean.example.com

I live in East Dean. It's a small village and it doesn't have big estates. It isn't next to the sea, so it doesn't have a pier or a marina. And it doesn't have a cinema. The children of East Dean don't go to school there: they go to school in Eastbourne. My parents don't work there because they work in Eastbourne too. My brother and sister don't like East Dean because it doesn't have a sports centre. But I like East Dean because it's my home.

b) (Circle) **the correct form: *doesn't* or *don't*.** *Kreise die richtige Form ein:* doesn't *oder* don't.

1 I doesn't / don't watch films in East Dean because it doesn't / don't have a cinema.

2 Young people doesn't / don't go to school in East Dean because it doesn't / don't have a secondary school.

3 East Dean doesn't / don't have many places and my parents doesn't / don't work there.

4 East Dean doesn't / don't have rubbish in its streets. Why? I doesn't / don't know why.

▶ Check

2 The lost bag

Write *don't* or *doesn't*. *Schreibe* don't *oder* doesn't.

Sunita Mum, where's my bag?

Meera You (1) _____ think it's in your room?

Sunita I (2) _____ know. But I know Nish sometimes takes my bag and he (3) _____ ask me. So I (4) _____ think it's in my room.

Meera Well, that (5) _____ help us now. Go and look in your room, Sunita.

Sunita You (6) _____ understand, Mum. Nish sometimes takes my things.

Meera But we (7) _____ know that Nish has your bag. Go and look in your room, Sunita!

Sunita Ah, here it is, Mum. Nish (8) _____ have it!

3 Zane and Noah are different

Write the sentences for Noah. *Schreibe die Sätze für Noah.*

> Remember!
> *She brushes her teeth.* → *He doesn't brush his teeth.*

1 Zane gets up at 7 a.m., but Noah doesn't _get up_ at 7 a.m.
2 Zane walks to school, but Noah doesn't _____ to school.
3 Zane has a sister, Holly, but Noah doesn't _____ as sister.
4 Zane takes Holly to school, but Noah doesn't _____ Holly to school.
5 Zane goes swimming, but Noah doesn't _____ swimming.
6 Zane watches TV, but Noah doesn't _____ TV.

▶ Check

4 Some students in my class

What's right? Circle the correct verb form. *Was ist richtig? Kreise die richtige Verbform ein.*

1 Radhia and Diya live / don't live on my estate.
2 Kiera goes / doesn't go to the youth centre.
3 Max reads / doesn't read a book.
4 Cindy cooks / doesn't cook for her family.
5 Luca does / doesn't do skateboarding.

5 Zara's new flat

Zane's friend Zara lives in London now. Write the right verb forms. *Zanes Freundin Zara wohnt jetzt in London. Schreibe die richtigen Verbformen.*

Hi, Zane. We're in our new flat. It's really good, but it doesn't _____ (1 have) a garden.

I _____ (2 have) a really nice room and I don't _____ (3 share) my room with my brother now!

We live near the shops, but I don't _____ (4 walk) there. I _____ (5 use) my bike.

One of our neighbours is a bit strange. She _____ (6 watch) me when I _____ (7 come) home, but she doesn't _____ (8 say) 'hello'.

Maybe she _____ (9 think) I'm weird! See you soon! Zara

▶ Check

6 Likes and dislikes

Look at the pictures. Then write the sentences. *Sieh dir die Bilder an und schreibe Sätze.*

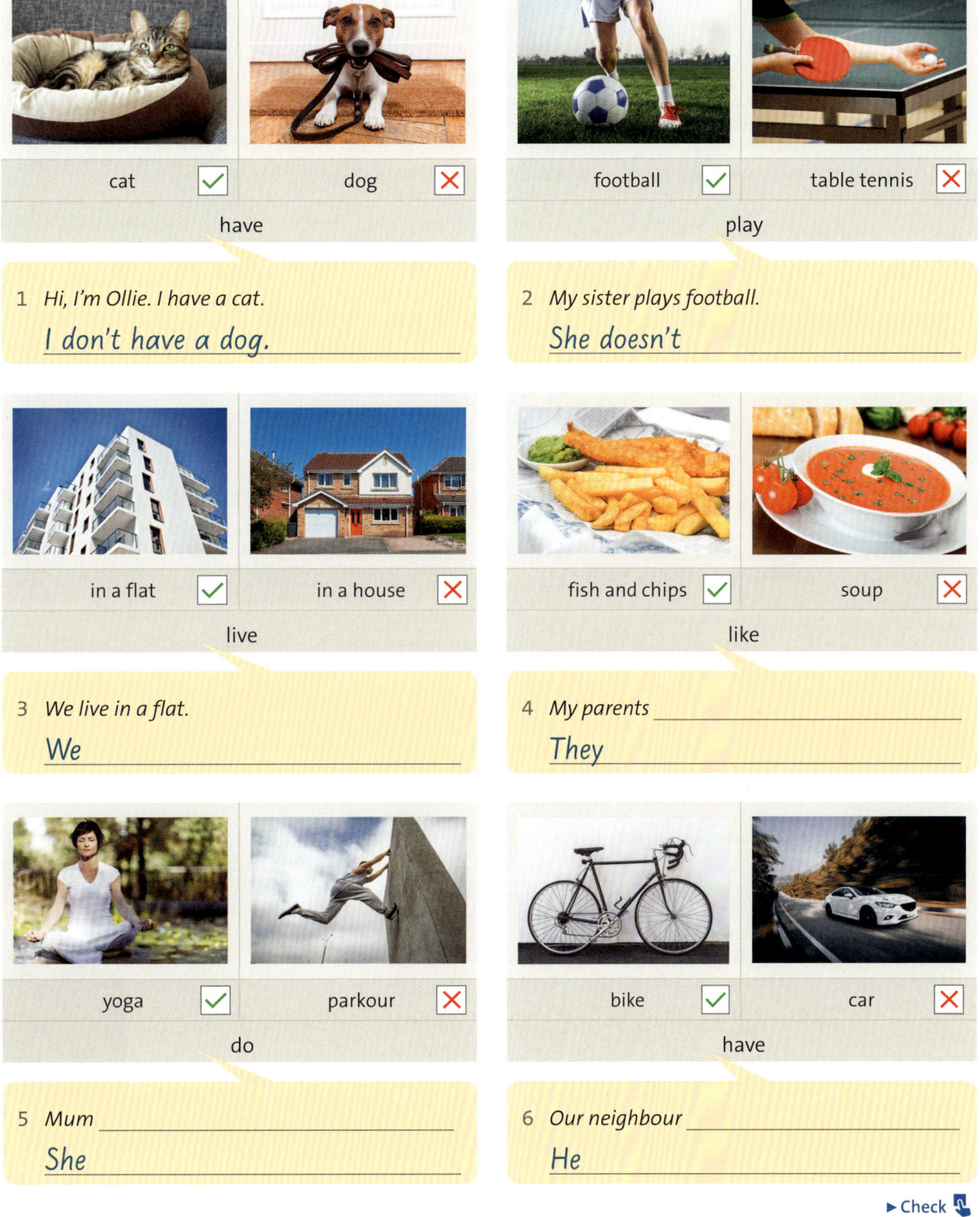

1 *Hi, I'm Ollie. I have a cat.*
   I don't have a dog.

2 *My sister plays football.*
   She doesn't

3 *We live in a flat.*
   We

4 *My parents* _____
   They

5 *Mum* _____
   She

6 *Our neighbour* _____
   He

▶ Check

4

Das simple present: Fragen und Kurzantworten

Fragen, die man mit „ja" oder „nein" beantworten kann, beginnen mit **Do** oder **Does**.

Es ist oft unhöflich, auf diese Fragen nur mit *yes* oder *no* zu antworten. Besser ist eine Kurzantwort.

| Do | I
you
we
they | + verb? | Yes, I do.
No, you don't.
Yes, we do.
No, they don't. | Does | he
she
it
my dad | + verb? | No, he doesn't.
Yes, she does.
No, it doesn't.
Yes, he does. |

Do you like bowling? Yes, I do. – Magst du Bowling? – Ja.
Do your parents speak English? – No, they don't. – Sprechen deine Eltern Englisch? – Nein.
Does the library open later? – Yes, it does. – Öffnet die Bibliothek später? – Ja.

▶ SB p. 111, pp. 180–181

7 Questions for you

Answer with *Yes, I do. / No, I don't.* or *Yes, it does. / No, it doesn't.*
Antworte mit Yes, I do. / No, I don't. oder Yes, it does. / No, it doesn't.

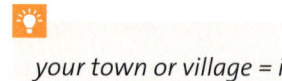
your town or village = it

1 Do you live in a village? – _____

2 Does your town or village have a station? – _____

3 Do you speak German at home? – _____

4 Does your house or flat have a garden? – _____

8 Questions about Lily

(Circle) **the right word in the questions.** *Kreise in den Fragen das richtige Wort ein.*

1 Do / Does Lily and her parents live on an estate? – Yes, they do.

2 Do / Does Lily's estate have some problems? – Yes, it does.

3 Do / Does Lily live with her sister? – No, she doesn't.

4 Do / Does Lily and her parents have friendly neighbours? – Yes, they do.

5 Do / Does Lily's dad sometimes walk in the park with Lily? – Yes, he does.

▶ Check

9 Saturday activities

a) Where do the people go on Saturdays? Circle the right word in the questions. *Wohin gehen die Leute samstags? Kreise in den Fragen das richtige Wort ein.*

b) Look at the map of Brighton and write the short answers. *Sieh dir die Karte von Brighton an und schreibe die Kurzantworten.*

1 Do / **Does** Grace go to the pier on Saturdays? – *Yes, she does.*

2 **Do** / Does Sam and Jo go shopping in the Lanes on Saturdays? – *Yes, they*

3 **Do** / Does Mr and Mrs Jones go to Jubilee Library on Saturdays? – *No, they don't.*

4 Do / **Does** Milan go to the Brighton i360 on Saturdays? – *Yes, he*

5 Do / **Does** Hannah go to St. Nicholas Rest Garden on Saturdays? – *No, she*

6 **Do** / Does Phil and his friends go to the station on Saturdays? – _____

7 Do / **Does** Norah go to the museum on Saturdays? – _____

8 **Do** / Does Amy and her dad go to the shopping centre on Saturdays? – _____

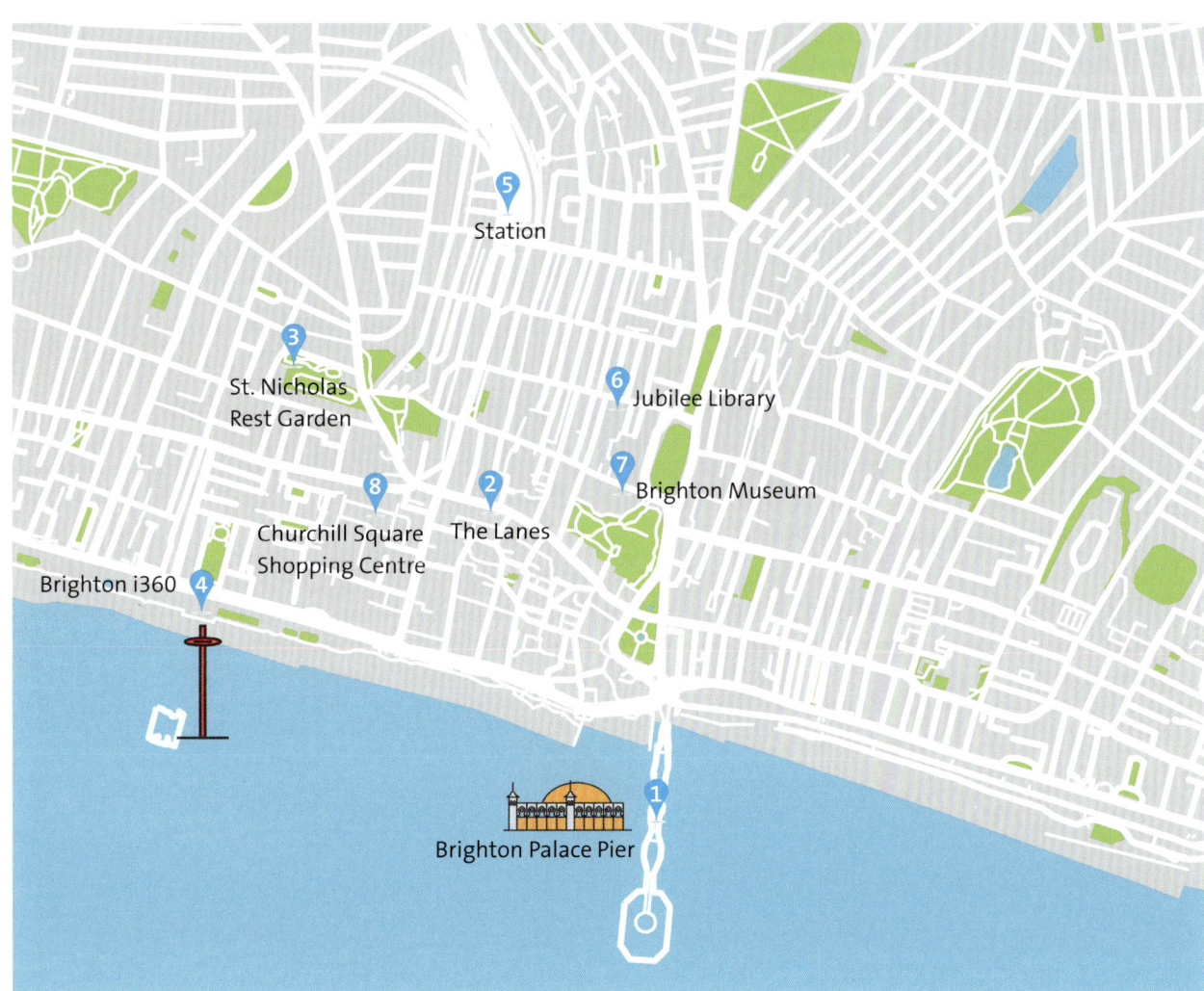

Das simple present: Fragen mit Fragewörtern

Auch Fragen mit Fragewörtern stellst du mit *do* oder *does*. Das Fragewort steht immer am Anfang.
Where do you live? – Wo wohnst du?
Why does she give us so much homework? – Warum gibt sie uns so viele Hausaufgaben?

Wenn du mit *Who?* oder *What?* nach dem Subjekt des Satzes fragst, bildest du die Frage ohne *do* oder *does*.
Who gets up first in your family? – Wer steht in deiner Familie als Erster auf?
What works best? – Was funktioniert am besten?

▶ SB p. 114, p. 181

10 Questions about school

Write questions. *Schreibe Fragen.*

1 How _____ you go to school? – By bus.

2 When _____ your first lesson start? – At 8.50.

3 Where _____ you have lunch? – In the canteen.

4 What _____ you do in your lunch break? – I talk with my friends.

11 More questions about school

Is the question correct? If yes, put a tick (✓). If it isn't correct, write the correct question.
Ist die Frage richtig? Wenn ja, setze ein Häkchen (✓). Ist sie nicht korrekt, schreibe die richtige Frage.

1	What do you bring to school?	_____
2	Where does Sunita do her homework?	_____
3	When do your sister go to school?	_____
4	What does you have for lunch?	_____
5	Who does Lily meet at school?	_____
6	How does Zane and Holly get to school?	_____

▶ Check

12 REVISION Brighton beach

Add -s or -es to the verb if necessary. *Ergänze -s oder -es am Ende des Verbs, wo nötig.*

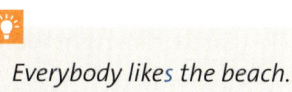
Everybody likes the beach.

I love _____ a summer's day on the beach. Everybody look _____ happy!

We bring _____ a picnic and sit _____ on the beach. Mum always go _____ swimming, but Dad doesn't swim _____ when it's cold. Then Mum read _____ a book and Dad do _____ a crossword. I listen _____ to music. In the afternoon we often go _____ to the pier and Dad buy _____ rock. The pier close _____ at 6 p.m., but we often don't want _____ to go home then.

13 REVISION At Hove Skatepark

Read Mailin's sentences. Write the missing words in Juri's sentences. *Lies Mailins Sätze. Ergänze die fehlenden Wörter in Juris Sätzen.*

can't • doesn't • don't • isn't

1 I like skateboarding.   I _____ like skateboarding.

2 I can skateboard very well.   I _____ skateboard very well.

3 Skateboarding is fun!   Skateboarding _____ fun!

4 My skateboard works well.   My skateboard _____ work well.

▶ Check

14 REVISION Weekends

Circle the right words. *Kreise die richtigen Wörter ein.*

Zane What do / does you do at the weekend?

Lily I don't / doesn't know. Mum often don't / doesn't want to go out. She want / wants to stay at home. But I sometimes go / goes out with Dad. And I often go / goes to the youth centre. What do / does you do at the weekend, Zane?

Zane I often cook / cooks for my family. They all like / likes that. Do / Does you cook in your family?

Lily No, I don't / doesn't.

15 REVISION Too many questions about the pier

Write the tourist's questions about the pier. Tip: Look at Zane's answers first!
Schreibe die Fragen des Touristen über die Pier. Tipp: Sieh dir zuerst Zanes Antworten an.

Are there • Can you • Do they • does it • Is it

Tourist _____ free to go on the pier?

Zane Yes, it is.

Tourist _____ trampolines?

Zane Yes, there are.

Tourist _____ have special activities at Halloween?

Zane Yes, they do. They have special activities at Halloween and also at Christmas.

Tourist _____ buy fish and chips on the pier?

Zane Yes, you can.

Tourist And when _____ close?

Zane It closes at 6 p.m.

Tourist Thank you. But it's cloudy and windy. I think it's too cold for the pier today!

▶ Check

Unit 5
Enjoy!

Das present progressive: Bejahte Aussagesätze

Erklärfilm

Mit dem *present progressive* sagst du, was jemand jetzt gerade tut. Du beschreibst damit auch, was auf Bildern passiert.

Das *present progressive* besteht aus zwei Teilen:
be + verb + -ing

Be kennst du bereits aus Unit 1.

I'm / am
you/we/they're / are   + verb + ing
he/she/it's / is

*She's look*ing *happy in the photo.* – Sie sieht glücklich aus auf dem Foto.
*I'm visit*ing *my grandma at the moment.* – Ich besuche gerade meine Großmutter.

▶ Grammarmaster p. 10, SB p. 138, p. 182

1 Noah's visit to London Zoo

a) **Noah and his grandma are in London Zoo. Circle the right form of the verbs.**
Noah und seine Großmutter sind im Londoner Zoo. Kreise die richtige Form der Verben ein.

1 I **'m** / 's taking lots of photos today.

2 Listen to the parrots! They **'re** / 's making a lot of noise!

3 Look! That big tiger! It 're / **'s** watching me!

4 And the visitors? They **'re** / 's enjoying the sun.

b) **Noah is on the phone to Zane. Complete his sentences with words from the two boxes.** *Noah telefoniert mit Zane. Vervollständige seine Sätze mit den Wörtern aus den beiden Kästen.*

Signalwörter für das *present progressive* sind *now* (jetzt, gerade), *at the moment* (im Moment), *today* (heute).

1
'm • 's • 're

+

2
eating • enjoying • standing • ~~visiting~~ • walking

1 I **'m   visiting** London with my grandma today.

2 We _____ _____ through London Zoo now.

3 I can see some elephants. They _____ _____ in some water.

4 A big crocodile is hungry. It _____ _____ some fish at the moment.

5 I _____ really _____ my time in London!   ▶ Check

5

Die *ing*-Form: Schreibung

Bei Verben, die auf *-e* enden, fällt das *-e* bei der *ing*-Form weg:

have – He's hav*ing* a shower right now.

share – I'm shar*ing* a room with my sister at the moment.

Bei einigen Verben wird der letzte Buchstabe verdoppelt:

plan – We're plan*ning* a great holiday.

sit – I'm sit*ting* in my room at the moment.

▶ SB p. 138, p. 182

2 Three activities

Write sentences. Use the verbs in box 2 in the correct form.
Schreibe Sätze. Verwende die Verben aus Kasten 2 in der richtigen Form.

1
are • 'm • is • 're • 's

+

2
eat • look • make (2x) • put • smile • write

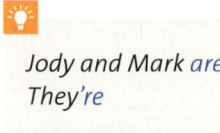

Jody and Mark *are*
They*'re*

Jo *is*
She*'s*

Look! Jody and Mark *are* _making_ a cake! They _____ strawberries on it.

Jo _____ happy. She _____ because her mum _____ her birthday cake.

I _____ an Indian dish, matter paneer. And my friend Kabir _____ _____ the recipe for me.

3 Double letters

Complete the verbs in the present progressive with *mm*, *nn*, *pp*, or *tt*.
Vervollständige die Verben im present progressive mit mm, nn, pp, *oder* tt.

1	I can see Steve. He's ru		ing to the shops.
2	Debbie is really fast. She's wi		ing her competition!
3	Where's Amina? – She's swi		ing in the sea.
4	Why are you si		ing in the classroom?
5	Oh, why is the car sto		ing here?
6	Great, the weather is ge		ing warmer!

▶ Check

56 fifty-six

Das present progressive: Verneinte Aussagesätze

Du verneinst die Formen von *be*.

I'm not
you / we / they aren't   + verb + ing
he / she / it isn't

I'm not going to school today. – Ich gehe heute nicht in die Schule.
Mum *isn't working* this week. – Mum arbeitet diese Woche nicht.

 Wie du *be* verneinst, weißt du bereits aus Unit 1.

▶ Grammarmaster p. 12, SB p. 138, p. 182

4 Meera and Ben are away one weekend

a) **What are the problems? Complete the sentences in the present progressive.**
Welche Probleme gibt es? Vervollständige die Sätze im present progressive.

not clean - kitchen

Sunita and Nish **aren't** _____

not work

The dishwasher[1] _____

not sleep

"I'm so worried about Sunita and Nish that I _____"

b) **Sunita is texting Meera. Complete her sentences in the present progressive.** *Sunita schreibt Meera. Vervollständige ihre Sätze im present progressive.*

Hi, Mum. Nish and I **are enjoying** _____ (1 enjoy) the weekend alone. I _____ (2 not get up) before ten and I _____ (3 not do) much. Nish is nice to me. He _____ (4 not take) my things. The animals _____ (5 eat) their food and they _____ (6 not make) much noise. Oh, but the dishwasher _____ (7 not work).

See you tomorrow!
Sunita

▶ Check

---
[1] **dishwasher** *der Geschirrspüler*

Das present progressive: Fragen

Um eine Frage im *present progressive* zu bilden, stellst du *be* an den Anfang des Satzes. Das Fragewort kommt noch davor.

What	am	I	
	Are	you / we / they	+ verb + ing
When	is	he / she / it	

What is Keira doing there? – She's doing yoga. – Was macht Keira da? – Sie macht Yoga.
Are you making a sandwich? – Yes, I am. – Machst du ein Sandwich? – Ja.

💡 Wie du Fragen mit *be* bildest, weißt du bereits aus Unit 1.

▶ Grammarmaster p. 17, SB p. 138, p. 182

5 What are you doing?

Answer the questions for you. Tick (✓) for "yes" and put ✗ for "no". *Beantworte die Fragen für dich. Mache ein Häkchen für „ja" und ein Kreuz für „nein".*

1 Are you sitting at a desk or table at home? ☐
2 Are you eating some sweets? ☐
3 Are the people near you making a lot of noise? ☐
4 Are you enjoying this exercise? ☐

6 What are they doing?

Match the questions and the answers. Draw lines. *Ordne die Fragen und Antworten zu. Zeichne Linien.*

💡 Die Kurzantworten beim *present progressive* sind dieselben wie beim Verb *be*.

1 Are you doing your homework? — Yes, they are.
2 Is Dad doing the shopping at the moment? — Yes, she is.
3 Are you and Hamza making lunch today? — Yes, I am.
4 Are Noah and Zane talking? — No, we aren't.
5 Is Sunita eating breakfast now? — No, he isn't.

▶ Check

7 A birthday party

a) **Complete the questions. Then look at the picture and write the answers.** *Vervollständige die Fragen. Schau dir dann das Bild an und schreibe die Antworten.*

 Um ein Bild zu beschreiben, verwendest du das *present progressive*.

1 _____ the girls _____ *having* _____ a birthday party (have)? – *Yes, they are.*

2 _____ it _____ (rain)? – *No, it isn't.*

3 _____ the girls _____ (smile)? – *Yes, they* _____

4 _____ they _____ birthday hats (wear)? – _____

5 _____ the girls _____ (sing)? – _____

6 _____ one girl _____ (eat)? – _____

b) **Look at the picture again. Complete the sentences.** *Schau dir das Bild noch einmal an. Vervollständige die Sätze.*

Helena *is having* _____ (1 have) her birthday party this afternoon. What

is _____ she _____ (2 do) for her party? Helena's friends

_____ (3 dance). But _____ Helena

_____ (4 dance) at the moment? She _____ (5 not dance)

because she _____ (6 eat). She _____ (7 watch) her friends

and she _____ (8 smile). Music _____ (9 play) and all the

girls _____ (10 have) fun.

▶ Check

5

much – many – a lot of

A lot of verwendest du in bejahten Sätzen. In Fragen und verneinten Sätzen verwendest du:

- **many** bei **zählbaren** Dingen. Du kannst von den Wörtern den Plural bilden, z. B. *one apple, two apples, …* Many bedeutet „viele".

  How many apples do we need? – Wie viele Äpfel brauchen wir?

  There aren't many people on the bus. – Im Bus sind nicht viele Leute.

- **much** bei **nicht zählbaren** Dingen. Du kannst von den Wörtern keinen Plural bilden, z. B. *time, music.* Much bedeutet „viel".

  How much ham do we have for our picnic? – Wie viel Schinken haben wir für unser Picknick?

  I don't have much time now. – Ich habe gerade nicht viel Zeit.

  ▶ SB p. 141, p. 183

8 Much or many?

a) **Write S if the words are singular, P if they are plural.**
Schreibe S, wenn die Wörter im Singular stehen und P, wenn sie im Plural stehen.

 Money beschreibt alles Geld zusammen. Du kannst es nicht zählen, sondern nur die einzelnen Münzen und Scheine.

| 1 bikes ☐ | 2 ballons ☐ | 3 flour ☐ | 4 men ☐ |
| 5 money ☐ | 6 people ☐ | 7 love ☐ | 8 time ☐ |

b) **Write the words from 8a) into the right list.** *Schreibe die Wörter aus 8a) in die richtige Liste.*

How much …?	How many …?

▶ Check

9 Questions about school

Read the questions about life at Varndean School and Ravi's answers. Circle the correct word.
Lies den Fragebogen über das Leben an der Varndean School und Ravis Antworten. Kreise das richtige Wort ein.

www.mywebsite.example.com

1 How do you go to school?

By bus. But there aren't much / many buses from our estate to town. So I usually stand.

2 Are school lunches OK?

The food isn't bad, but I think the problem is that we don't get much / many time to eat it.

3 Is homework OK?

It's OK. We often don't get much / many homework. That's good.

4 Is sport a problem at school?

Yes, it is. It think we don't do many / much sport at school.

5 Do you feel happy at school?

Usually yes. But I think it's maybe hard for students who don't have much / many friends.

10 Quiz

Complete the questions with *much* or *many*. Then guess and tick (✓) the right answers. You can check your answers online. *Vorvollständige die Fagen mit* much *oder* many. *Rate und hake die Antworten ab. Du kannst die Lösungen im Internet überprüfen.*

1 How _____ players are there in a rugby team?
 A eleven ☐ B fifteen ☐

2 How _____ food does an elephant eat in a day?
 A 50 to 60 kilos ☐ B 150 to 160 kilos ☐

3 How _____ rain does London get?
 A about the same as Paris ☐ B more than Paris ☐

▶ Check

4 How _____ colours does a rainbow have?
   A five ☐   B seven ☐

5 How _____ people live in Britain?
   A over 65 million ☐   B under 55 million ☐

6 How _____ time can a game of cricket take?
   A three to five hours ☐   B three to five days ☐

11 Lily and Zane's picnic

Lily and Zane are preparing a picnic. *Lily und Zane bereiten ein Picknick vor.*

a) Look at the pictures and write Zane's questions with *How much* and *How many*. *Sieh dir die Bilder an und schreibe Zanes Fragen mit* How much *und* How many.

b) Write Lily's answers with *much* or *many*. *Schreibe Lilys Antworten mit* much *oder* many.

1 Zane How *many* _____ eggs do we have?
   Lily There aren't *many eggs.* _____

2 Zane How *much* _____ ham do we have?
   Lily There isn't *much ham.* _____

3 Zane How _____ carrots do we have?
   Lily There aren't _____

4 Zane How _____ sausages do we have?
   Lily There aren't _____

▶ Check

12 REVISION Verbs

Write the verbs into the right list. *Schreibe die Verben in die richtige Liste.*

~~go~~   make   swim   stop   buy   run
look   take   give   dance   enjoy   sit

help → helping	write → writing	get → getting
go → going		

13 REVISION What are you doing, Noah?

Write questions. *Schreibe Fragen.*

1. What _are_ you _doing_ (do), Noah? – I'm going to Lily's birthday party.
2. Who _____ (go) with you? – Buddy is going with me.
3. What _____ you _____ (take) in your bag?
   – A present for Lily, Buddy's favourite ball, my phone, …

✉ 15 REVISION And you?

a) **Are the sentences true for you? Tick (✓) for "yes" or put (✗) for "no".** *Treffen die Aussagen auf dich zu? Mache ein Häkchen für „ja" und ein Kreuz für „nein".*

1. I'm doing my homework. ☐
2. My parents aren't helping me. ☐
3. My little brother is playing in the living room. ☐
4. My cat is sleeping on my bed. ☐

b) **Write four more sentences about what you are or aren't doing or what people near you are or aren't doing. Use the present progressive.** *Schreibe vier Sätze darüber, was du gerade tust oder nicht tust oder was die Menschen um dich herum gerade tun oder nicht tun. Verwende das present progressive.*

▶ Check

Auf einen Blick

Unit 1 My new school

▶ Grammarmaster p. 4

Der unbestimmte Artikel: *a/an*

Der unbestimmte Artikel (ein, eine) heißt im Englischen **a** oder **an**.
Du verwendest
- **a**, wenn das folgende Wort mit einem Konsonanten (b, c, d, …, z) beginnt,
  a boy – ein Junge   a car – ein Auto
- **an**, wenn das folgende Wort mit einem Vokal (a, e, i, o, u) beginnt.
  an animal – ein Tier   an exercise book – ein Heft

! Substantive (*boy, car, rabbit*) schreibst du (anders als im Deutschen) klein.

▶ SB p. 21, p. 175

▶ Grammarmaster p. 5

A/an vor Vokalen

Vorsicht bei vorgeschobenen Adjektiven, die mit einem Vokal (a, e, i, o, u) beginnen.
I have a dog. It's an old dog. – Ich habe einen Hund. Er ist ein alter Hund.

Bei der Wahl von **a** oder **an** ist die Aussprache entscheidend, nicht die Schreibweise, also:

    a uniform – eine Uniform   … weil das gesprochene Wort am Anfang
    a unit – eine Lerneinheit   wie *you* klingt
Aber: *an hour – eine Stunde*   … weil das „h" am Anfang nicht gesprochen wird

▶ SB p. 21, p. 175

▶ Grammarmaster p. 5

Der bestimmte Artikel: *the*

Du sprichst den bestimmten Artikel **the** (der, die, das):
- [ðə], vor einem Wort, das mit einem Konsonanten beginnt: *the [ðə] teacher, the [ðə] car*
- [ði], vor einem Wort, das mit einem Vokal beginnt: *the [ði] animal, the [ði] apple*

▶ SB p. 21, p. 175

▶ Grammarmaster p. 6

Der Plural der Nomen

An die meisten Nomen wird im Plural **-s** angehängt.

a dog → two dogs – ein Hund, zwei Hunde

a cat → three cats – eine Katze, drei Katzen

! Sonderformen:
one child → two children – Kind / Kinder
one man → two men – Mann / Männer
one woman → two women – Frau / Frauen

Ein paar wenige Nomen haben keine Singularform und werden nur im Plural gebraucht:
people – Menschen   *trousers – Hose*   *clothes – Kleidung*

▶ SB p. 22, p. 175

Auf einen Blick

▶ Grammarmaster p. 7

Der Plural der Nomen: Formen

Die Folgenden sind die drei wichtigsten Pluralformen:

1. die meisten Nomen + **-s**
   a lion → two lions
   a year → three years

2. **-s, -x, -ch** oder **-sh** + **-es**
   a bus → two buses
   a beach → two beaches

3. **Vokal + y + -s**
   a boy → two boys

   Konsonant + y wird zu **-ies**
   a story → two stories
   a pony → two ponies

▶ SB p. 22, p. 175

▶ Grammarmaster pp. 8–9

Die Personalpronomen

Personalpronomen ersetzen Nomen (z. B. table → it) oder Eigennamen (z. B. Ben → he).
Die Personalpronomen sind:

I (ich) we (wir)
you (du, Sie) you (ihr, Sie)
he (er) they (sie)
she (sie)
it (es)

❗ Das Pronomen **I** (ich) wird im Englischen immer **groß**geschrieben.
Das Pronomen **it** steht für Dinge und Tiere und entspricht „er", „sie" oder „es":
I have a guitar. ~~The guitar~~ It's great.
What page is it?

▶ SB p. 24, p. 176

▶ Grammarmaster pp. 10–11

Erklärfilm

Das Verb *be*: Bejahte Aussagesätze

Es gibt zwei Formen von **be**: Kurzformen *(short forms)* und Langformen *(long forms)*. Bei den Kurzformen ersetzt ein Apostroph (') einen weggefallenen Buchstaben.

	Langformen	**Kurzformen**	
• bei offiziellen Schreiben	I am	I'm	• beim Sprechen
• nach Eigennamen *(Zane, Sunita)*	you are	you're	• in persönlichen E-Mails oder Chats
• nach Nomen *(bike, teachers)*	he is / she is / it is	he's / she's / it's	• nach Pronomen: *(I, you, he, she, it, we, you, they)*
	we are	we're	
	you are	you're	
	they are	they're	

▶ SB p. 24, p. 177

▶ Grammarmaster pp. 12–13

Erklärfilm

Das Verb *be*: Verneinte Aussagesätze

Bei der Verneinung von **be** benutzt du fast immer die Kurzform.

I'm not very big.
You aren't very big.
He isn't very big.
She isn't very big.
It isn't very big.
We aren't very big.
You aren't very big.
They aren't very big.

▶ SB p. 29, p. 177

sixty-five **65**

Auf einen Blick

▶ Grammarmaster p. 14

Der s-Genitiv

Mit dem s-Genitiv drückst du aus, dass etwas zu jemandem gehört.

Singular *(Noah, Mr Lee)*	's	*Noah's dog* – Noahs Hund
		Mr Lee's class – Herr Lees Klasse
Plural mit -s *(boys, Watsons)*	s'	*the boys' phones* – die Handys der Jungen
		the Watsons' house – das Haus der Watsons
Plural ohne -s *(men, women)*	's	*the men's clothes* – die Kleidung der Männer
		the women's cars – die Autos der Frauen

▶ SB Hello! + Unit 1, p. 174

▶ Grammarmaster p. 15

Die *of*-Fügung

Gehören zwei Sachen zusammen, verbindest du sie mit *of*.
the end of the story – das Ende der Geschichte

Of verwendest du auch bei Mengenbezeichnungen.
a kilo of oranges – ein Kilo Orangen

▶ SB Hello! + Unit 1, p. 174

Auf einen Blick

Unit 2 My family and home

▶ Grammarmaster pp. 17–19

Das Verb *be*: Fragen und Kurzantworten

Erklärfilm

Bei Fragen steht *be* am Anfang des Satzes.

You *are* English. → *Are* you English?   She *is* brave. → *Is* she brave?

Antworte auf eine Frage nicht einfach mit *yes* oder *no*. Das klingt unhöflich. Verwende Kurzantworten.

Fragen	Kurzantworten
Am I right?	Yes, *you are*. / No, *you aren't*.
Are you tired?	Yes, *I am*. / No, *I'm not*.
	Yes, *we are*. / No, *we aren't*.
Is Freya nice?	Yes, *she is*. / No, *she isn't*.
Is it late?	Yes, *it is*. / No, *it isn't*.
Are Tim and Lisa happy?	Yes, *they are*. / No, *they aren't*.

▶ SB p. 47, p. 178

▶ Grammarmaster p. 20

There is ... / There are ...

Mit *there is* (*there's*) und *there are* sagst du, dass etwas vorhanden ist. Im Deutschen heißt es meist: Es gibt ..., Da sind ..., Es stehen ..., Da liegen ...

Du verwendest:

- *There's* ... mit dem Singular
  There's a cat in our kitchen. – Da ist eine Katze in unserer Küche.
  Is there a toilet here? – Yes, *there is*. – Gibt es hier eine Toilette? – Ja.

- *There are* ... mit dem Plural
  There are three bedrooms in our flat. – Es gibt drei Schlafzimmer in unserer Wohnung.
  Are there lots of people here? – Yes, *there are*. – Gibt es hier viele Menschen? – Ja.

▶ SB p. 50, p. 178

▶ Grammarmaster p. 21

Die Possessivbegleiter

Possessivbegleiter zeigen an, wem etwas gehört.

I	→	*my* sister – meine Schwester	we	→	*our* kitchen – unsere Küche
you	→	*your* house – dein Haus	you	→	*your* car – euer Auto
he	→	*his* clothes – seine Kleider	they	→	*their* bedroom – ihr Schlafzimmer
she	→	*her* laptop – ihr Laptop
it	→	*its* colour – seine/ihre Farbe

!

- *it's* = it is: *It's* cold today. – Es ist kalt heute.
  its = sein, ihr: our garden with *its* trees – unser Garten mit seinen Bäumen

- *they're* = they are: *They're* German. – Sie sind Deutsche.
  Their = ihr(e): Here are Dan and Jo with *their* dad. – Hier sind Dan und Jo mit ihrem Vater.

▶ SB Units 1–2, p. 176

Auf einen Blick

Unit 3 My day

▶ Grammarmaster pp. 23–25

Das simple present

Erklärfilm

Mit dem *simple present* sagst du, was oft, jeden Tag oder nie passiert.

    I / you / we / they play
he / she / it / my sister plays   **!** *He, she* und *it*, das *-s* muss mit!

Häufige Signalwörter im *simple present* sind: *always* (immer), *often* (oft), *sometimes* (manchmal), *never* (nie).

▶ SB p. 80, p. 179

▶ Grammarmaster p. 26

Das simple present: Sonderformen

Es gibt im *simple present* ein paar Sonderformen bei *he/she/it*:

- -ss, -x, -sh, -ch oder -o + -es:

  brush: He brushes his teeth.   go: She goes to school.

  watch: My sister watches TV.   do: My dad does parkour.

- Konsonant (b, c, d, ... z) + y wird zu -ies: tidy: My brother tidies his room.

- have → has: Our flat has three bedrooms.   ▶ SB p. 80, p. 179

▶ Grammarmaster pp. 27–28

Die Wortstellung

In Aussagesätzen ist die Wortstellung: **subject** – **verb** – **object**.

Dad	makes	dinner		when	he	comes	home from work
Papa	macht	das Abendessen,		wenn	er	von der Arbeit nach Hause	kommt.

Mit Häufigkeitsadverbien (*always, often, sometimes, never*) kannst du sagen, wie oft etwas geschieht. Anders als im Deutschen stehen sie im Englischen meist direkt vor dem Hauptverb.
We sometimes play a game. – Wir spielen manchmal ein Spiel.   ▶ SB p. 83, p. 179

Auf einen Blick

Unit 4 Where I live

▶ Grammarmaster pp. 46–49

Das simple present: Verneinte Aussagesätze

Um Aussagen im *simple present* zu verneinen, verwendest du don't oder doesn't.

| I
you
we
they
my parents | + don't + verb | | he
she
it
my brother | + doesn't + verb |

I don't like maths. – Ich mag Mathe nicht.
My mum doesn't work in town. – Meine Mutter arbeitet nicht in der Stadt.
We don't play cricket. – Wir spielen nicht Cricket.

▶ SB p. 107, p. 180

▶ Grammarmaster pp. 50–51

Erklärfilm

Das simple present: Fragen und Kurzantworten

Fragen, die man mit „ja" oder „nein" beantworten kann, beginnen mit Do oder Does.
Es ist oft unhöflich, auf diese Fragen nur mit *yes* oder *no* zu antworten. Besser ist eine Kurzantwort.

| Do | I
you
we
they | + verb? | Yes, I do.
No, you don't.
Yes, we do.
No, they don't. | Does | he
she
it
my dad | + verb? | No, he doesn't.
Yes, she does.
No, it doesn't.
Yes, he does. |

Do you like bowling? Yes, I do. – Magst du Bowling? – Ja.
Do your parents speak English? – *No, they don't.* – Sprechen deine Eltern Englisch? – Nein.
Does the library open later? – *Yes, it does.* – Öffnet die Bibliothek später? – Ja.

▶ SB p. 111, pp. 180–181

▶ Grammarmaster p. 52

Erklärfilm

Das simple present: Fragen mit Fragewörtern

Auch Fragen mit Fragewörtern stellst du mit *do* oder *does*. Das Fragewort steht immer am Anfang.
Where do you live? – Wo wohnst du?
Why does she give us so much homework? – Warum gibt sie uns so viele Hausaufgaben?

Wenn du mit *Who?* oder *What?* nach dem Subjekt des Satzes fragst, bildest du die Frage ohne *do* oder *does*.
Who gets up first in your family? – Wer steht in deiner Familie als Erster auf?
What works best? – Was funktioniert am besten?

▶ SB p. 114, p. 181

Auf einen Blick

Unit 5 Enjoy!

▶ Grammarmaster p. 55

Erklärfilm

Das present progressive: Bejahte Aussagesätze

Mit dem *present progressive* sagst du, was jemand jetzt gerade tut. Du beschreibst damit auch, was auf Bildern passiert.

Das *present progressive* besteht aus zwei Teilen:

be + verb + -ing

I'm / am
you/we/they're / are   + verb + ing
he/she/it's / is

💡 *Be* kennst du bereits aus Unit 1.

She's looking happy in the photo. – Sie sieht glücklich aus auf dem Foto.
I'm visiting my grandma at the moment. – Ich besuche gerade meine Großmutter.

▶ Grammarmaster p. 10, SB p. 138, p. 182

▶ Grammarmaster p. 56

Die ing-Form: Schreibung

Bei Verben, die auf *-e* enden, fällt das *-e* bei der *ing*-Form weg:

have – He's having a shower right now.

share – I'm sharing a room with my sister at the moment.

Bei einigen Verben wird der letzte Buchstabe verdoppelt:

plan – We're planning a great holiday.

sit – I'm sitting in my room at the moment.

▶ SB p. 138, p. 182

▶ Grammarmaster p. 57

Das present progressive: Verneinte Aussagesätze

Du verneinst die Formen von *be*.

I'm not
you / we / they aren't   + verb + ing
he / she / it isn't

💡 Wie du *be* verneinst, weißt du bereits aus Unit 1.

I'm not going to school today. – Ich gehe heute nicht in die Schule.
Mum isn't working this week. – Mum arbeitet diese Woche nicht.

▶ Grammarmaster p. 12, SB p. 138, p. 182

Auf einen Blick

▶ Grammarmaster pp. 58–59

Das present progressive: Fragen

Um eine Frage im *present progressive* zu bilden, stellst du *be* an den Anfang des Satzes. Das Fragewort kommt noch davor.

What	am	I	
	Are	you / we / they	+ verb + ing
When	is	he / she / it	

💡 Wie du Fragen mit *be* bildest, weißt du bereits aus Unit 1.

What is Keira doing there? – She's doing yoga. – Was macht Keira da? – Sie macht Yoga.
Are you making a sandwich? – Yes, I am. – Machst du ein Sandwich? – Ja.

▶ Grammarmaster p. 17, SB p. 138, p. 182

▶ Grammarmaster pp. 60–62

Erklärfilm

much – many – a lot of

A lot of verwendest du in bejahten Sätzen. In Fragen und verneinten Sätzen verwendest du:

- many bei zählbaren Dingen. Du kannst von den Wörtern den Plural bilden, z. B. *one apple, two apples, …* Many bedeutet „viele".

  How many apples do we need? – Wie viele Äpfel brauchen wir?
  There aren't many people on the bus. – Im Bus sind nicht viele Leute.

- much bei nicht zählbaren Dingen. Du kannst von den Wörtern keinen Plural bilden, z. B. *time, music*. Much bedeutet „viel".

  How much ham do we have for our picnic? – Wie viel Schinken haben wir für unser Picknick?
  I don't have much time now. – Ich habe gerade nicht viel Zeit.

▶ SB p. 141, p. 183

Grammatical terms *(Grammatische Fachbegriffe in diesem Heft)*

adjective	das Adjektiv: *good, old, nice, …*		positive	die positive Form: *do, can, …*
adverb (of frequency)	das (Häufigkeits-)Adverb: *often, always, sometimes, never*		possessive determiner	Possessivbegleiter: *my, your, his, her, its, our, their*
article	der Artikel: *a / the* book *an / the* apple		present progressive	die Verlaufsform der Gegenwart: *I'm speaking*
form	die Form		short answer	die Kurzantwort: *Yes, I do. / No, I'm not. / Yes, she does. / …*
long form	die Langform: *I am, do not, you are*		short form	die Kurzform: *I'm, don't*
negative	die negative Form: *don't go, can't go, aren't going, doesn't go, …*		simple present	die einfache Gegenwart: *I speak English, he likes it*
noun	das Nomen/Substantiv: *friend, car*		statement	Aussage(satz)
object	das Objekt: *I like cats.*		subject	das Subjekt: *They eat dinner.*
personal pronoun	Personalpronomen: *I, you, he, she, it, we, they*		verb	das Verb: *(to) go, (to) do, (to) have, (to) think, (to) love, …*
plural	Plural, Mehrzahlform: *books, children, potatoes, stories, …*		wh-question	die Frage mit Fragewort: *What's this? Who are you?*

Quellenverzeichnis

Titelbild
Cornelsen/Personen: Cornelsen/Anja Poehlmann, Brighton Pier: mauritius images/Steve Vidler

Illustrationen
Cornelsen/Evelt Yanait (Umschlaginnenseite vorne (U2), Abb. S. 4; S. 4 1–8; S. 6 un.mi.; S. 12 1–6; S. 14 A–D; S. 15 1–5; S. 18 1–6; S. 19 1–6; S. 20 mi.; S. 24 1–6; S. 53 mi.; S. 56–57; S. 59; S. 60; S. 62 1–4)

Abbildungen
Umschlaginnenseite vorne (U2), Abb. S. 64**:** Shutterstock.com/Studio Ayutaka; **S. 3** Cornelsen/Anja Poehlmann; **S. 6** ob.mi.: Shutterstock.com/Studio Ayutaka; **S. 7** m.re.: Shutterstock.com/Zurijeta; **S. 8–9** Cornelsen/Anja Poehlmann; **S. 11** ob.re.: Cornelsen/Oliver Meibert, m.li.: Shutterstock.com/Denis Kuvaev, un.li.: Shutterstock.com/dotshock; **S. 13** mi.: stock.adobe.com/Daniel; **S. 15** un.re.: Imago Stock & People GmbH/OceanPhoto; **S. 16** un.re.: stock.adobe.com/Monkey Business; **S. 16** un.re.: stock.adobe.com/Monkey Business; **S. 21–23**: Cornelsen/Anja Poehlmann; **S. 25** ob.re.: stock.adobe.com/Johnstocker; **S. 26** un.re.: Shutterstock.com/Hasan Shaheed; **S. 27 mi.li.:** Shutterstock.com/valeryvoronessa, **un.re.:** Shutterstock.com/Juice Flair; **S. 28 un.mi.:** Shutterstock.com/VH-studio; **S. 45 li.:** Shutterstock.com/Upl; **S. 46 mi.re.:** Shutterstock.com/AVM Images; **S. 47** un.li.: Cornelsen/Anja Poehlmann; **S. 48** un.mi.: Shutterstock.com/TheHighestQualityImages; **S. 49** cat: Shutterstock.com/Iva Vagnerova, dog: Shutterstock.com/Javier Brosch, football: Shutterstock.com/Fotokostic, table tennis: Shutterstock.com/dwphotos, flat: Shutterstock.com/Grand Warszawski, house: Shutterstock.com/Ewelina W, fish and chips: Shutterstock.com/Anna Mente, soup: Shutterstock.com/Martin Rettenberger, yoga: stock.adobe.com/Copyright: all rights reserved, michaeljung@163.com/michaeljung, parkour: Shutterstock.com/areporter, bike: Shutterstock.com/YL Stock, car: stock.adobe.com/Ivan Kurmyshov; **S. 50** un.re.: Cornelsen/Anja Poehlmann; **S. 51** (Collage): Alle Shutterstock.com: Karte: Ink Drop, Kartenmarkierungen: oculo, Brighton Sehenswürdigkeiten (Palace Pier und tower): iconim; **S. 54** mi.re.: stock.adobe.com/ingusk; **S. 60** bikes+men+flour+ballons+time: Shutterstock.com/Pogorelova Olga, money+people+love: Shutterstock.com/Jemastock; **S. 61** rugby+rain: Shutterstock.com/Peterdraw, elephant: Shutterstock.com/Kastoluza; **S. 62** rainbow: Shutterstock.com/0DIS0, people: Shutterstock.com/Kastoluza, cricket: Shutterstock.com/aresdimahdiss; **S. 64** un.li.: Shutterstock.com/Studio Ayutaka